Job
Relocation

ANTHONY G. MUNTON

NICK FORSTER

YOCHANAN ALTMAN

LINDA GREENBURY

Job Relocation

Managing People on the Move

JOHN WILEY & SONS

Chichester · New York · Brisbane · Toronto · Singapore

Other Wiley Editorial Offices

John Wiley & Sons, Inc., 605 Third Avenue,
New York, NY 10158-0012, USA

Jacaranda Wiley Ltd, G.P.O. Box 859, Brisbane,
Queensland 4001, Australia

John Wiley & Sons (Canada) Ltd, 22 Worcester Road,
Rexdale, Ontario M9W 1L1, Canada

John Wiley & Sons (SEA) Pte Ltd, 37 Jalan Pemimpin #05-04,
Block B, Union Industrial Building, Singapore 2057

Library of Congress Cataloging-in-Publication Data

Job relocation : managing people on the move / Anthony G. Munton ... [et al.].
    p.   cm.
    Includes bibliographical references and index.
    ISBN 0-471-93728-2
    1. Employees—United States—Relocation.   I. Munton, Anthony G.
HF5549.5.R47M34   1992
658.3'83—dc20   92–23725
                                                              CIP

British Library Cataloguing in-Publication Data

A catalogue record for this book is available from the British Library

ISBN 0-471-93728-2

Typeset in 11/13pt Palatino from authors' disks by Text Processing Department,
John Wiley & Sons Ltd, Chichester
Printed and bound in Great Britain by Biddles Ltd, Guildford, Surrey

For the McKeons: thanks for the Kev Test

CONTENTS

AUTHOR ADDRESSES

Dr Anthony G. Munton
MRC/ESRC Social and Applied Psychology Unit
Department of Psychology
University of Sheffield
Sheffield   S10 2TN
England

Dr Nick Forster
Cardiff Business School
University of Wales College of Cardiff
Aberconway
Collum Drive
Cardiff   CF1 3EU
England

Dr Yochanan Altman
Lyon Graduate School of Business
Lyon
France*

Ms Linda Greenbury
Director
Career Development Centre for Women
97 Mallard Place,
Twickenham
Middlesex   TW1 4SW
England

---

* Contact address: 262 Shakespeare Tower, Barbican, London EC2Y 8DR, England
Tel/Fax 071 628 9419

FOREWORD

Relocation is probably the only area of human resource management in which employers must give consideration to the needs of the family, not just the employee. For when employees are asked to relocate—be it a domestic transfer to an unfamiliar environment involving separation from family, friends and social support networks, or an international assignment with the added dimensions of a different culture and possibly an unknown language—the move will have a dramatic effect on a wide circle of people beyond the employee. The requirement to move impacts on the whole family. Spouses, children, other dependent relatives—all may suffer, emotionally and financially, as a result of the decision to move.

Some employers may believe that their duty is to the employee, and the employee alone. However, it is increasingly being recognized that damaged family relationships—disaffected spouses who have given up careers, children upset and unable to settle at school, family concerns over aged relatives left behind and the unhappiness and loneliness associated with the loss of friendships—will affect the employee's performance at work. It is difficult to divorce domestic dissent and poor quality home life from the working environment, even for the most dedicated of company employees.

Traditionally, organizations have taken a nuts and bolts approach to relocation management, concentrating heavily on housing issues and the practicalities of moving people from A to B. How best to fund the relocation from a cost effective standpoint has been the prime concern. Critics have suggested that employers may "throw money at the problem", the principle being that money will remove employees' concerns and reduce (or eliminate) any resistance to relocation.

Money cannot simply be thrown at people, however, in the mistaken belief that the consequence will be the elimination of the problem. Of course money helps to sweeten the pill—for a dual income couple, for example, it can help to reduce the period of financial uncertainty when one job is lost on relocation—but it cannot replace other tangible losses: a career for the spouse, a good education for a child who is settled in school, good job prospects for older children in a particular area and so on.

Although it is true that over the years relocation policies have tended to become more complex with a burgeoning array of allowances for all manner of eventualities, employers have never really been in a position to "throw money" at employees. Cost effectiveness is crucial to all areas of company business—and the human resources department is no exception. Indeed, in today's cost conscious times when competitiveness is the key to success (domestically and globally) a balance must be struck between the need to "buy out" problems and to find alternative cost effective solutions. Spending their way out of difficulty cannot provide employers with the answer to their employee mobility problems—both because employees are likely to remain dissatisfied and because cost constraints prevent such action anyway—so employers have had to seek out alternative approaches.

Practical help has been identified as an effective means of reducing employee/family stress and, in turn, resistance to moving. Practical assistance in the form of the provision of advice, information, counselling and so on, resulting in greater involvement in the process of change, can significantly reduce employees' and their families' genuine fears and concerns over such issues as educational and career options for family members.

Human resources professionals can often find themselves under pressure from employees with family and housing dilemmas—but being philanthropic is not the answer. Human resources departments have a duty to their organizations although it is still possible for them to respond to employees' needs. A policy of effective relocation assistance, practical help and a caring approach is required. Together such courses of action can prove to be sufficient to ensure mobility and a settled employee and family unit.

Employers are not simply moving an employee but are uprooting whole families—with all the associated repercussions. The information on good practice in this book will provide a valuable guide for all those involved in the process of relocation.

Sue Shortland
Manager
CBI Employee Relocation Council

PREFACE

Job relocation describes a situation in which an employee is asked to move themselves, and more often than not their family, to another geographical area in response to a request from their employer. These simultaneous house and job moves are becoming increasingly common in the UK. In a report published in 1987, the Institute for Manpower Studies estimated that 250 000 employees make moves of this kind every year. Multiply that figure to include other family members, and it is likely that up one million people are relocating within the UK each year. To that figure can be added the several thousand people involved in international relocations every year.

The financial cost to UK companies of domestic and international relocation has put the issue fairly and squarely into the consciousness of even the most sceptical of company directors. At an estimated £30 000 per move for domestic relocation, and a few thousand more for an overseas move, British industry is probably spending in the region of eight *billion* pounds a year on relocating its employees for one reason or another.

For many people, regular relocation comes with the job. Those who choose to pursue a career in areas such as retail management, the financial services sector, or the hotel and catering trade, do so with the expectation that promotion and relocation are likely to go hand in hand.

In recent years, these people have been joined by those involved in what have become known as corporate, or group, moves. With regional changes in commercial property prices and office rents, and improvements in electronic and telecommunications, many organizations have found it viable to move their entire operations away from high cost areas such as the South East. The result has been something of an exodus from London and its surrounding areas to new locations. Popular destinations have included places such as Reading, Swindon and down the M4 corridor towards Bristol. Other organizations, most notably the Civil Service, have moved northwards to Nottingham, Sheffield, Leeds and the North West.

As the numbers of people relocating grew, so a volatile property market pushed up the cost to employers. Not surprisingly, the reaction was one of extreme concern. One result has been the establishment, and expansion of, the Confederation of British Industry's (CBI) Employee Relocation Council (ERC). Boasting several hundred member organizations, the ERC provides a popular and effective forum for discussing the complex issues that surround job relocation.

Initially, the concern among employers centred on the costs and benefits associated with establishing and maintaining relocation packages. While these issues remain a priority, increasing interest has been expressed in the human side of relocation management. The question so often asked is: "Why, when we are spending in the region of £30 000 for each move, are so many people experiencing difficulties when they relocate?"

Employers are all too aware of the fact that stress resulting from relocation can have a significant impact on an employee's work. They also know that where relocation related stress becomes extreme, people will look for alternative employment. Rising rates of refusal and increased labour turnover are both tangible signs of the problem. These concerns, and others like them, have led to a growth in social science research aimed at improving our understanding of the problems experienced by relocating employees and their families.

During the process of working with organizations, and talking to employees and their families, the authors have frequently been asked whether they know of any practical guide to this human aspect of relocation. The expressed desire has been for a publication that would do two things: first, reliably inform relocation practitioners about the range of problems encountered by employees and their families, and put forward suggestions as to how those problems might be tackled; and second, provide a readable, accessible manual that would offer relocating employees and their families practical guidance in understanding and coping with their own thoughts and feelings.

To this end, what follows is a consideration of the human side of relocation from the perspective of the relocating employee and his or her family, and from the perspective of those responsible for managing company relocation policy.

Chapter 1 (Job relocation and the family) looks at the relationship between work and home life in a general way, tackles the issue of just how stressful relocation can be for people, and considers the causes of that stress, and what employees and their families want from their relocation packages.

Chapter 2 (Organizational aspects of job mobility and relocation: a guide for personnel managers) takes the perspective of those responsible for managing relocation. The need for a mobile workforce is considered in conjunction with the aim of keeping the potential disruption of job change and relocation to a minimum.

Chapter 3 (Women and relocation) discusses the increasingly important issue of the professional and personal problems faced by relocating women. All of the available research points to the fact that not only are more women being relocated by their organizations, but also more relocating men have women partners with their own full-time careers. This represents a significant social change that demands urgent attention.

Chapter 4 (Corporate relocations: a jigsaw puzzle in human resource management) concerns the managerial problems inherent in executing a large group move. From planning the announcement to post-relocation reactions, the chapter deals with the potential problems and pitfalls of a major organizational change.

Chapter 5 (International aspects of job relocation in the 1990s) tackles the issue of why and how multinational organizations use international moves as part of their corporate strategy, the impact that these moves have on employees and their families, and how good management can minimize the risks to all concerned.

Finally, Chapter 6 (Check-list for successful relocation) offers a summary of the practical advice given throughout the book. The aim is to provide a user-friendly guide for relocating employees and their families.

Nick Forster
Tony Munton

ACKNOWLEDGEMENTS

Much of the research work referred throughout the book was undertaken over a four-year period whilst Nick Forster and Tony Munton were employees of the Medical Research Council (MRC) at the Social and Applied Psychology Unit (SAPU), Sheffield University. We would like to thank MRC and our former colleagues at SAPU for their invaluable support and practical help over that period. Many thanks also to Dr Robert Stratford of the University of Southampton for access to his work on relocation and education.

Yochanan Altman has undertaken his research on corporate relocations while with the Cranfield School of Management. Cranfield Institute of Technology, and he would like to thank the Graduate Research Committee for their financial support. Also special thanks to David Jackson from Australia for his dedicated field work during the spring and summer of 1991.

CHAPTER 1 Job relocation and the family

INTRODUCTION

In this chapter, we look at how relocation can have a very real impact on the lives not just of employees, but of their families as well. The first section deals with the general issue of how work and family life are bound up with each other. Should British companies get involved in developing policies with the family in mind?

The second section deals with the problem of stress. What is it, what causes it and how can individuals, and employers, help to reduce the stress involved in relocation?

Next, the results of a large scale investigation into job relocation are used to analyse which aspects of relocation people find most stressful, and what might be done by employers to help them.

Finally, the views of relocating employees and their partners are used to make some practical suggestions as to how company relocation policy needs to change if it is to reduce to a minimum the risk of stress.

WORK AND FAMILY LIFE

What have family issues got to do with the world of commerce and industry? To many managers and executives in Britain the traditional answer has been "nothing". Employers are concerned only with what goes on during working hours. What happens outside of the working day is the private affair of employees. Contrast that attitude with the experience of corporations in the USA: for example, the engineering company with 120 000 employees and 127 full-time counsellors operating a 24-hour, seven days a week counselling service with an annual budget of over one million dollars. The reply of one well known British entrepreneur to the suggestion that we might follow that example is not untypical: "We don't go in for that crap here".

So who is right? Are American corporations paternalistic to a degree which would be unacceptable in Britain, or are companies in the UK simply failing to recognize a need for, and financial advantages of, greater involvement with problems facing employees and their families?

For many people, modern industrialized society can produce a conflict of interest between the demands of work and the demands of home. This section looks at ways in which this conflict can arise, and the impact it can have on employees, on their families, and on the corporations that employ them. Finally, some practical examples of how successful British companies are developing solutions to this problem are provided.

The Relationship between Work and the Family

Research evidence shows quite conclusively that, for most people, what goes on at work has a very direct impact on the personal lives of both themselves and their families. The number of hours worked, and how those hours are scheduled are obvious examples. Those fortunate enough to have the freedom to choose their own methods of working and their own timetables often find it much easier to meet family responsibilities and so tend to be more satisfied with family life.

A dramatic example of the disruption faced by families as a result of the demands of work comes from research into job relocation carried out by the Social and Applied Psychology Unit (SAPU) at Sheffield University. Every year an estimated 250 000 people are asked to move by their employers. Multiply that figure to include members of the family, and you end up with close on one million people relocating annually in Britain. For around half of all those involved the impact on their lives produces stress of some kind.

This can manifest itself in a variety of ways, from loss of sleep and irritability, to feelings of guilt and inadequacy that can be a serious threat to psychological health.

The process is one that works in both directions. What goes on away from the office can also influence attitudes and behaviour at work. Rose Kanter, organizational guru of the American corporate scene, comments: "family situations can define work orientations, motivations, abilities, emotional energy, and the demands people bring into the workplace". Several people interviewed in the course of our relocation research explained that the resentment building up at home not just towards the move, but towards the company as well, was making them seriously consider the possibility of looking for a new job.

However, not all people are the same. Although it is often tempting to make generalizations, people have very different ways of dealing with the relationship between work and home life. Some prefer to keep the two very separate. Worries about work are left at the office at five o'clock and not discussed at home. Others may see life in one domain as compensating for the tribulations of the other. Commitment to a full family life can compensate for frustrations or disappointments at work. Perhaps most common is the tendency for incidents or feelings built up at work to spill over into home life, and vice versa. How often have you shouted at your partner/child/cat on coming home because of something that happening during your day at work?

Many working people experience a real and uncomfortable sense of conflict between commitment to their careers on the one hand, and commitment to their families on the other. Inevitably, involvement in one has to be limited in order to accommodate the demands of the other. The inner turmoil that this creates can have serious implications for both the individual concerned and their employer. Increased risk to physical health among employed parents, less satisfaction with life and oneself, and poorer mental health are common results. Lower productivity, high rates of absenteeism and labour turnover, and poor morale are all side effects that cost employers money. What follows is an example of the kind of conflict that can arise as the result of a badly managed relocation.

Andy is the manager of a large food store belonging to one of the High Street chains. He has recently been promoted, which involved a relocation from North Yorkshire to Essex. His wife, Julia, worked for an estate agent, but the move meant her having to give up her job. It also meant her moving away from her mother who was widowed two years previously. Six months after moving into their new home, Julia has still not found a new job and is becoming increasingly miserable about having left friends and family. Because Andy is having to work late most evenings, the couple have had little opportunity to get to know new people since moving. When interviewed, Andy commented:

> At the moment I feel work is making me neglect my home life. That makes me very angry, especially when I go home and see the state my wife is in. If they could have you in there 24 hours a day they would, and I don't think that's a good way to run things. As it stands it's not all that difficult for me to get work with one of the other retail food chains. I know the company spent a lot on my training, but if they don't show a bit more understanding on this, what choice will I have? I'm not going to lose my wife for the sake of the job.

It is also an established fact that the work/home conflict is often more acute and more disabling for women. We live in a society which, on the whole, readily condones men neglecting many of their family and domestic responsibilities in order to go to work. The same society puts women in the position of being expected to have a greater commitment to their homes and families than to their careers. This evidently makes climbing the corporate ladder that much harder for women. Whatever you may read in your favourite style magazine about the "new man", research findings are quite consistent: while women develop new career responsibilities outside the home, there is little or no redistribution of roles at home. Women are commonly put in the unenviable position of being expected to maintain two jobs, one at work and another at home.

Social Change and the Shift in Attitudes

It would be nice to think that society in general, and men in particular, will one day wake up to the inequity of this situation. No doubt change will come. Indeed, it may be happening at a faster rate than many realize. In a survey published recently in the *Guardian*, 64% of people questioned in the UK believed that the most satisfying marriages were those in which both partners were in paid employment.

There is little doubt that we are seeing a change in attitudes. Gone is the egocentric, make money at all costs, "lunch is for losers" philosophy of the eighties. This is the age of the Social Charter, of freedom from motorway cones and trains that run on time. In the caring, sharing, nineties, quality of life is the new currency. For example, research into job relocation has shown at least one in three managers refusing promotions that involve a move because of family commitments and responsibilities. People are becoming increasingly less willing to make decisions about work that will have any unfavourable impact on the family.

In the previous decade, working long hours was the badge of the single minded, ambitious manager. It was a virtue to be in the office before eight in the morning and still there after eight at night. Never mind the impact on quality of family life. We even had a Prime Minister renowned for her ability to work twenty hours a day. But how efficient or effective is it to work that hard? Do we really want people on the verge of burn-out making important economic and political decisions that can influence all our lives? Can people who have to spend all those hours at work be doing their jobs properly?

A recent survey of European managers suggests that working shorter hours can actually improve productivity. In which European country would you expect to find managers working the shortest hours? The answer is Germany. The most successful Euro economy has recognized the benefits of having 35–45 hours of productive time each week from a happy, healthy manager rather than 70–100 hours from someone whose ability to work is inevitably clouded for much of the time. To coin an old phrase, "It's not the hours you put in, but what you put into the hours".

However, it's not only changing attitudes that demand the attention of Great Britain plc. There are important demographic changes that also need to be considered. The next decade is going to witness dramatic increases in the numbers of working women. The Employment Department estimates that over 50% of all new managerial posts created between now and the end of the century will be filled by women. The inevitable consequence is an equally dramatic rise in the numbers of dual career couples in the economy. Currently in the USA only 7% of all families conform to the traditional stereotype of working husband, non-working wife and children. Britain is not far behind. We know from our own work in the relocation field that over 70% of managers surveyed had partners in employment. The majority of those working partners were people with their own careers. They were not "cake-winners" with part-time jobs that bought the family little luxuries once in a while.

Human Capital and Cost Effectiveness

So far we have established that conflict between work and family is a reality, that it is often more of a problem for women than men, and that demographic and social changes are likely to bring these issues into a much sharper focus. The question remains as to what employers should be doing in response. Should they get involved with their employees' lives away from the work-place at all?

The short answer to that particular question is that employers are very much involved with family life already. Corporate policy on issues like relocation or working hours has a very direct impact on family life. The problem is that while organizations are quite prepared to make decisions that have a negative impact on the family, they often deny responsibility for taking more positive action on the grounds that this would amount to interference. The logic is evidently flawed.

Apart from any moral obligation, employers have sound economic reasons for taking an interest in the family lives of their employees. An organization stands or falls on the quality, not of its product, but of its people. Human capital is the single most valuable investment that any organization has. Its product is simply the collection of the physical and intellectual efforts of its employees. It makes no difference whether that product is a sheet of steel, a desktop computer or a newspaper. No amount of investment in the latest high tech machinery will guarantee success if the people responsible for the machines are not working effectively.

To get the best out of their most valuable asset, employers need to put the best in. No organization would spend tens of thousands of pounds on a piece of equipment without drawing up and sticking to a programme of regular maintenance. Similarly, having invested heavily in the recruitment and training of personnel, employers need to be aware of what is happening to that person both at work and in the wider social context, and offer support when and where it is appropriate or necessary. A caring attitude on the part of an employer engenders positive attitudes in employees, loyalty being one of the most important. Having a loyal work-force means greater efficiency and more effective long-term planning.

Very soon, employers may be faced with less choice in the matter. People are becoming more scarce. Fewer people combined with fewer opportunities for training is already leading to some talk of a skills shortage. As the race to recruit the best new talent intensifies, organizations perceived as being sensitive to the wider needs of their employees are likely to prove the more popular.

Good Practice in British Companies

What are the options for organizations wanting to develop policies more sensitive to the needs of the family? In general the first step is a commitment to communication. Developing policies responsive to the needs of employees presupposes some awareness of those needs. Some means by which employees can communicate their needs to their employers, and vice versa, are essential.

Examples of the range of employee benefits on offer are typically taken from corporate practice in the USA. They include parental leave (both maternity leave and "daddy breaks"), childcare provisions, eldercare programmes, flexible working hours and locations, employee counselling, and career development without the need for relocation. Each has obvious and positive benefits for family life.

Reviews of the movement towards greater employee care often cite the development of Employee Assistance Programmes (EAPs) in the USA as the starting point. Originally instigated as a response to rising absenteeism due to alcohol abuse, EAPs have become synonymous with the idea of employers providing counselling and help with problems that may originate outside of work. However, it would be a mistake to think that this whole concept originated in the USA. The great Victorian industrialists such as Cadbury, Rowntree and Lever Brothers were not slow to realize the benefits of taking physical and psychological care of employees and their families. Bournville, Port Sunlight and other model towns like them are testaments to that philosophy.

Even today, only 20% of all companies in the USA offer parental leave anything over and above the minimum required by law. At the same time there are plenty of examples of enlightened corporate practice among successful British companies.

For British Petroleum, providing day-time childcare facilities for employees has been found to be extremely cost effective. Being able to retain women employees within the company saves on the considerable costs of recruiting and retraining new personnel. Given that replacing an employee costs up to one and a half times that person's annual salary, the potential savings are evident.

National Westminster Bank has found career breaks to be another effective way of retaining valued women in the organization. Women are encouraged to take up to five years away from the company, usually to start a family. Keeping careers open in this way has resulted in a return rate of some 50%. The saving on investment in human capital makes the scheme cost effective.

Finally the Body Shop, perhaps not coincidentally headed by a woman, is another example of a British company with progressive policies. The provision of childcare facilities, encouraging husband and wife teams to work within the company, giving people paid leave to work on community and voluntary projects, and partnership and profit sharing schemes are all evidence of a commitment to quality of family life.

Summary

Social changes mean that people are attaching greater importance to the quality of their family life. The conflict that people face when confronted with the competing demands of work and family is a serious issue. Employers have an economic interest in becoming more aware of both the impact that this conflict can have on employees, and the impact that corporate policy has on family life. Contrary to popular myth, not all good company practice in this area is to be found in America. There are plenty of examples of positive family orientated policies working well in British companies. This is undoubtedly encouraging, not just for employees and their families but for employers too. Successful organizations are often characterized as those able to respond, with flexibility, to changes in their markets. Success towards the end of the twentieth century will also depend on a similarly flexible approach to changes in social attitudes towards the importance of family life.

RELOCATION AND STRESS

How Much of a Problem is Stress?

The research evidence concerning the incidence of stress among relocating employees and their families is quite consistent. Roughly half of those involved in a move experience at least some of the symptoms commonly associated with stress. On a more positive note, that also means that around half of all those relocating do so with little or no trouble. The different experiences and attitudes people have are neatly summed up by these two extracts from our research interviews:

> I quite like moving. The rapid turnover of people, new colleagues, new job, new house. I don't worry about leaving friends or family. I quite like moving.

> You always worry about a move. Having made mistakes before, you worry that you might be making mistakes again. You just don't know until you've been there for six months.

Of course, it's worth bearing in mind that in any random sample of people there will be a certain proportion who will be experiencing some difficulties in their lives due to other circumstances. However, taking that proportion into consideration, compared with random samples three times as many relocating employees and four times as many relocating partners report experiencing symptoms associated with stress. For one in three people, these symptoms persist six months after moving into their new homes.

This next section examines in a general way what we mean by stress, how it is caused, how to notice the signs and symptoms in ourselves and others, and what might be done to deal with it.

What Is Stress?

Stress has a lot in common with indigestion. It's one of those notions that everybody has heard of, many have experienced, but few can define. It is perhaps one of the most researched topics in medicine and the social sciences. Despite its common usage among both lay people and the scientific community, the fact of the matter is that there is no single definition of stress. However, before looking at some of the particular aspects of relocation that can create stress for employees and their families, we need to establish what is meant by "stress".

The text books usually begin by referring to the Latin word *stringere*, translated as "to draw tight". This is not altogether a bad place to start. The image of someone under stress feeling tense or strung out is quite a common one. From this point, the word "stress" came to be promoted in modern language, most probably through its use in the engineering field where stress is associated with pressure or external force. Pressure in the form of an external force is exerted on a structure or small part of it, putting it under stress. If the structure copes with the pressure, all well and good. However, if the pressure becomes too great, the structure can break or crack under the strain, causing a complete collapse. Although these are all engineering terms, the way in which they have been adopted in the description of people is self-evident.

The engineering analogy of stress has a great deal of common-sense appeal. However, like many ideas promoted as common sense, there is a little more to it than that. Research has shown quite clearly that not all people react in the same way to similar situations. Relocation is a case in point: "Everybody knows that moving house is stressful". However, our surveys have consistently demonstrated that around five out of every ten relocatees experience few or no symptoms of stress. What might be pressure to one person may be seen as a stimulating challenge by another. People do not behave in the same predictable way as machine parts. The difference is that people can interpret pressure in ways that inanimate objects do not. The engineering analogy needs modifying.

A definition of how stress can influence people needs to recognize the fact that two people can interpret a similar situation in completely different ways. The more demanding a situation is seen to be, the more likely it is that signs of stress will appear.

How Is Stress Caused?

What makes a situation demanding and thus potentially stressful for person A but not for person B? Interpretation. In any potentially stressful situation, the person involved makes two assessments or judgements. First, how much pressure will this situation put me under? Second, do I have the ability and external resources necessary to cope with that level of pressure? When these two things are in balance, stress is not a problem. However, if a situation is interpreted as involving more pressure than the person believes they can cope with, then feelings of helplessness, of being unable to control events, can produce stress. Beliefs about control are commonly associated with stress. This is an important principle in the context of relocation that will be discussed in more detail when we look at what organizations can do to make the process easier for employees and their families. For the moment it is worth noting that when people feel they can at least have some influence over events, they are less likely to find a situation stressful.

What physical reactions commonly occur when an imbalance between assessment of pressure and availability of necessary coping resources takes place? The result is similar to any situation in which we have little or no control over some potential danger or threat. Consider a common example like taking off in an aeroplane.

Physiologically, the body prepares itself for action. Heart rate increases to provide more oxygen for muscles. Levels of sugar and fat in the blood are increased to provide more energy. Blood vessels in the stomach and skin shrink in order to divert more blood to the brain and muscles. Sweat is produced to cool the skin down. Blood thickens in preparation for possible clotting to repair wounds. Under normal circumstances, this state of alert does not last for long and is followed by action and then relaxation. However, where stress is prolonged, sustained increases in heart rate, blood sugar and blood fat levels can damage the body. High blood pressure, heart attacks, peptic ulcers and migraine are just some of the physiological conditions associated with stress.

Psychologically, the effects of being in this state of tension for long periods are equally serious. Lack of sleep, poor appetite, reduced ability to concentrate and feeling anxious or frightened are common symptoms. All of these serve to further reduce the ability to cope with pressure and so further increase feelings of stress. Performance at work suffers, personal relationships with colleagues, family and friends become fraught, and poor levels of attention make accidents more likely.

The question "what is stress?" is evidently very closely linked to the question "what causes stress?" It is difficult to provide an answer to one without answering the other. However, an answer can be provided. Not a definitive answer, but at least one that can be useful in understanding the effects that relocation can have on people. Stress describes a psychological and physiological reaction to a situation assessed as involving more pressure than one has the ability or external resources to deal with.

Things to Watch For: The Signs of Stress

Looking for the signs of stress in ourselves or others is extremely important during periods of potential upheaval like relocation. The earlier the signs and symptoms are identified, the sooner problems can be addressed and the less likely they are to become serious. While many of these symptoms can be recognized in others, it is often more difficult to spot them in ourselves. Some of the physiological and psychological reactions to stress have been discussed already. Increased nervousness, irritability, indecision, poor memory, loss of appetite, insomnia and complaints about aches and pains are all early signs. However, sometimes people can disguise or repress these early signs by using a variety of temporary coping mechanisms. These "defence mechanisms" are strategies people use in order to avoid facing up to the source of their discomfort. While a comprehensive review of all the different strategies people use is inappropriate here, a case study will help to illustrate the point.

Case study

Peter is a sales manager in the office of a relocating company. In his mid-twenties, he is married with one young son. Educated up to university degree level, he came to the company as a graduate entrant. His progress through the organization has been as expected for someone of his age and ability. He has worked in the same location for five years. However, the company is relocating its offices which entails a house move of 120 miles or so, from London to the south-west. Because the move is one involving the entire company, there is no automatic promotion involved for Peter. He feels that while his career prospects with the company are good, the move will mean being considerably further away from other potential employers, restricting his long-term options. Differences in property prices would make a return to London difficult.

Peter has the reputation of being friendly and easy to work with. Colleagues have remarked to his line manager that Peter has become extremely irritable at work. He seems to look very tired and is having to put in longer hours than usual in order to do the same amount of work. Careless errors are starting to creep into what is normally a fastidious approach to the job.

Whenever he comes into contact with members of either the company relocation team or the external relocation agency, he becomes quite hostile. Although the move is

continued ┘

continued

fast approaching, he seems to be making very little effort to find a new house. Peter is well aware of the situation but appears to take a very cavalier attitude of "everything will be OK", as if it was someone else rather than himself making the move.

Without anything other than a commitment to keep lines of communication open, this information would be readily available to those responsible for managing the move. Peter is showing a number of signs that he is failing to cope as well as he might. He is becoming uncharacteristically irritable with colleagues. He looks tired and is perhaps having to work longer hours because of difficulties in concentrating on his work. An increase in the rate of errors he makes supports this hypothesis. His unwarranted hostile attitude towards members of the relocation team suggests that he is *displacing* his aggression on to them. He feels angry with someone, but can only express it by becoming aggressive with colleagues. His lack of commitment to finding a new house is like some form of *denial* that the move is actually taking place. Finally, Peter's detached attitude suggests that he is again trying to avoid confronting the real implications of his situation.

Had someone taken the time to talk to Peter, they might have discovered some of the problems that the relocation is posing for him at home. His wife, Mary, does not want to move. She has spent many years living in London and consequently her immediate family all live quite locally. She has a particular dislike for the area to which they are moving and is convinced they will be forced to live on a modern estate. Her career in the public sector will not be enhanced by the sideways move she will be forced to make, if she is able to find a job at all, that is. The nearer the move comes, the more depressed she becomes, and the more aggressive towards her husband.

Of course it is important to remember that not everybody will experience difficulties when relocating. Indeed, the case history above is probably an extreme example. The point to remember is that signs of stress, even the less obvious ones, can be quite easily recognized in ourselves and in other people. However, this entails both a will to look out for these signs and commitment to maintaining active communication with those involved in a relocation.

How to Help: Looking After Yourself

Many of our ideas about stress rely heavily on the engineering analogy discussed earlier. In that model, mechanical breakdown occurs because of some structural fault in a vital component. When this mechanical explanation is applied too literally to people, stress can sometimes appear to be the result of some personal failing or weakness. It is probably more appropriate to view stress as the result of people being put into situations that they should never be asked to deal with. The fault lies in the situation rather than within the person. However, the fact is that these faulty situations do arise from time to time. When they do, there are practical steps that people can take to increase their chances of coping successfully.

As noted earlier, feeling that a situation is under control goes a long way to reducing the threat of stress. Many of the self-help strategies commonly discussed lay particular emphasis on learning to take control of your own physical and mental functioning. The importance of monitoring personal health and behaviour, recognizing the signs of stress in oneself, has already been dealt with. Other useful skills include learning how to relax quickly and effectively, recognizing the importance of physical exercise and knowing when and how to seek support from friends and family.

This is evidently not the place to go into detail about how to cope with personal stress. However, there are several very good books that do just that. For example, in *Living with Stress*, Cary Cooper Rachel Cooper, and Lynn Eaker look at sources of stress at work and at home, and offer practical advice on how to deal effectively with them.

How To Help: What Employers Can Do

When discussing what makes a situation stressful, it was noted that people make two assessments or judgements. First, how much pressure will this situation put me under? Second, do I have the ability and the necessary external resources to cope with that level of pressure? If the situation is interpreted as involving more pressure than can be dealt with, people feel that they are no longer in control of events, and the result is stress. What can the relocation manager do to reduce the risk of this happening?

The answer is in two parts. First, make sure that people are provided with what they need in the way of external resources. This not only helps relocating employees and families to cope with stress, but can often reduce the possibility of the problem arising at all. Second, help employees and their families to re-interpret, or reassess both the pressure involved in their situation and their own ability to cope with it. This may involve anything from an informal chat to the provision of professional counselling, depending on the seriousness of the problem.

The importance of employees and their families maintaining a sense of control over their relocation has been a recurring theme when discussing stress management. In order to achieve control, people need to know what will happen, when it will happen, and what they can do to influence it. In other words, they need the right information at the right time, and they need to be able to talk over their reactions with someone responsible for managing the move.

Research has shown that employees reporting symptoms associated with stress often feel that they have not had adequate opportunity to discuss their move with those responsible for managing it. A recent survey showed one in every three employees to be less than satisfied with communication between relocation managers and themselves.

It is a similar story when it comes to the quality of information provision. Maintaining a sense of control over the process is an important aspect of coping with a move. If employees are not being given adequate information when they need it, they are more likely to feel powerless and hence stressed. Survey results again show one in three employees to be less than satisfied with information provision during the early stages of a move.

Communication policy needs to be carefully thought out in advance. It should aim to keep rumour to a minimum and remove as much uncertainty from the minds of employees as possible. The most important thing to remember about communication is that it is a two-way process. It is not just a matter of the organization telling employees what is happening. Providing the opportunity for employees to talk about their concerns to the employer is just as important.

Providing adequate advance notice of a move is also important. People need time to prepare. Without that time, their feelings of loss of control can be reinforced. Generally speaking, the more notice people have, the less likely they are to experience stress.

The role of overload, especially at work, has been cited as a major factor in stress. During this time of upheaval and change for the whole family, employers can also help by keeping unreasonable work demands to a minimum. Consideration at this stage makes the transition easier, and hence the period of adjustment shorter.

Finally, during the latter stages of the relocation process help of a more general kind may be required. As employees and their families try to adjust to their new lives, new problems can arise. After the novelty of the new house and surroundings has worn off, people are left to face the reality of their situation. Living in a strange city, no friends, the children not settling into their new school, the new boss not being approachable. During times such as these, old family problems can suddenly become magnified. Relationships can become strained. It may be that in some cases the services of a professional counsellor are called for. Unless the relocation manager has been in regular contact with the employee, the situation may pass unnoticed. Communication, dialogue and flexibility are just as important at this later stage.

Summary

Stress has been described as a psychological and physiological reaction to a situation assessed as involving more pressure than one has the ability or external resources to deal with. Recognizing the early signs of stress is an important first step in helping either yourself or others. Once identified, a variety of different self-help strategies can be employed to deal with the problem. Many of these action plans have to do with learning how to take control, either of oneself or the problem. Employers can also play their part in helping to reduce the potential for stress during relocation. This can be achieved by encouraging employees and their families to maintain a sense of control over the process through adequate provision of information, a commitment to communication and taking a flexible approach to service provision.

WHAT ASPECTS OF RELOCATION DO PEOPLE WORRY ABOUT?

This section is based on the findings of a two-year research project undertaken by SAPU at the University of Sheffield. The research, funded by the Medical Research Council and the Economic and Social Research Council, involved following over two hundred relocating employees, and their families, through the whole relocation process. The first contact with people was made as soon as they had agreed to accept a relocation. Subsequent follow-ups took place three months after people had moved into their new homes, and again three months after that. At each of these three points in time, questionnaires were completed by employees and by their partners. In addition to the questionnaires, a number of interviews were conducted with people in their own homes.

Although relocating employees and their partners tended to worry about different aspects of the move at each of the three different survey points, four major issues dominated: property, children, family and social life, and work. Each of these will be dealt with in turn.

Property

Consistent with findings from an earlier pilot study, the research showed that issues surrounding the buying and selling of property were the most common cause of concern for relocating employees and their partners. As with many people who move home, it was those services provided by estate agents and solicitors that provoked much of the adverse comment from those relocating. However, the following are issues more specific to job relocation.

Will we find something suitable?

During the early stages of relocation, the worry is whether or not a suitable home can be found in the new location. A very important element in concerns of this kind is the amount of time people are given to look for a new home. Employers vary in the extent to which they will give people time off work to search for a house. Some organizations try to help their employees by offering a variety of home search services. These can vary from local estate agents posting out details of everything available, to a third party collecting information about individual requirements and then searching for something more specific. However, respondents in our sample were not altogether very positive when asked to rate how helpful they had found these services. That is not to assume that the quality of these property search services was not good. The negative response is more likely to be a reflection of the fact that most people like to be personally involved when it comes to choosing where to live. Buying a house is the single biggest purchase that most of us make, and one that has an enormous impact on the quality of our lives. To leave the decision to a third party may provoke feelings of a lack of control that can lead so easily to stress. The lesson for employers is that giving people adequate time to house-hunt can have a significant impact on reducing the worry of being able to find a suitable home. Where home search services are offered, employees and their partners should be consulted as to the kind of service they would find most useful.

Buying and selling

Anyone who has ever bought their own home will be aware of the potential sources of worry involved. Employers offer a range of services to make the process as easy as possible, but for many people this will still be the most stressful aspect of their move. On the plus side, those elements of a relocation package designed to help with property transfer are the most commonly offered and most gratefully received. Over 90% of our research sample received assistance with solicitors' and surveyors' fees, financial assistance with removal costs, and settling in costs. The majority found help of this sort extremely useful.

A relatively recent innovation has been the advent of the relocation management company. These organizations offer a range of services including familiarization tours of a new area, advice on local schools, and employment counselling for relocating partners. The results of our research indicate that the majority of employers use relocation companies to provide at least some of the services on offer to employees. The most commonly provided service is some variation of a *home sale guarantee scheme*. Although the details vary from one relocation company to another, the essence of these schemes is that the employee receives a guaranteed price for their old property, making them, in effect, first-time buyers in the new location. The attraction of these schemes is that the employee is freed from the burden of being trapped in a "property chain", at least on the selling side. However, a word of caution is called for. In their efforts to release the employee from any of the worry concerning the sale of their home, relocation companies can sometimes actually do too much. Bearing in mind the relationship between stress and feelings of being in control, it is important that employees feel they are still in charge of the sale. For that reason, a good relocation company will make every effort to keep the employee, and their partner, regularly informed throughout the home sale process. Provision of a personal service by staff who are aware of the stresses and strains employees and their partners may be under is the essence of a successfully administered home sale guarantee scheme.

Can we afford to live there?

Towards the latter stages of relocation, concerns about moving into higher cost housing areas become more acute. This problem was particularly common during those periods when the housing market was very volatile, with prices rising virtually on a weekly basis. In response to this problem, the majority of employees are offered a mortgage subsidy or its equivalent when relocation involves a move to a higher cost area. Not surprisingly these schemes are rated as very helpful by those concerned.

The Effects of Relocation on Children

It is quite clear from our research that the effects of relocation on children are a major cause of concern. Parents worry most about the impact of moving on educational development. These comments from a manager with a sixteen-year-old son are typical of those made in interviews:

> My wife and myself could live anywhere... we can just get up and go. It's my son that I'm worried about. I'm worried about his schooling. Are we unsettling him? Will he still get to university? What effect might the move have on that? I've got all that on my conscience.

Concern was also commonly expressed regarding children's social welfare:

> I'm most worried about my daughter's new school. Getting her to and from there, the quality of education and whether she can make a friend quickly. She's seen new girls coming into her school, and how they can get bullied, so she's quite apprehensive.

Guilt is one of the common emotions mentioned by parents in this context. It is not unusual for people to feel guilty about forcing the move on their children. That can have obvious implications for stress and ultimately on the way in which people do their jobs. Attitudes towards the employer are also likely to be affected. This can involve a lack of co-operation with the move, resistance to any further moves and even expressed wishes to leave the company. In an atmosphere where parents feel hostile and concerned about a relocation so early on, there is a real prospect of this concern being transferred to children. Already apprehensive, parental attitudes can serve to heighten any anxieties children may have and ultimately make adaptation and adjustment more difficult.

There is without doubt a popular truism that says changing schools is bad for children. However, work carried out by Dr Robert Stratford at the University of Southampton suggests that the picture is not quite that simple. A review of the research literature shows that there is little in the way of conclusive evidence to show that moving schools harms children in any consistent manner.

The effects that a change of school may have on children have been examined under three headings: friendships, social adjustment and educational attainment.

Friendships

Many researchers agree that this aspect of going to a new school is, for many children, often more important than the academic side of things. Children attending a new school can feel very alienated and alone. Unsure about new rules, even the most outgoing can take on the appearance of being chronically shy under these conditions. When asked what worried them most about an up-and-coming move, children put loss of friends at the top of their lists. As with adults, the lack of close friends can add significantly to the discontent associated with moving. Feeling miserable and lonely will only hinder the process of adjustment to a new environment.

There is some evidence that children tend to over-estimate the extent to which they will have trouble making new friends. Even where difficulties do exist, they are, for many, only short term. However, it is worth noting that age can play a large part in how successful children are in developing new peer relationships. Adolescents in particular find it difficult to break into what are often very close knit groups at this age. Similarly, the direction of a move has a significant influence. Children moving from a rural to an urban environment, or vice versa, may find it more difficult to make new friends.

Social adjustment

Moving from a familiar environment to a strange new place can have an impact on how a child behaves, particularly on an emotional level. While the process of adjustment runs its course, there may be noticeable differences in behaviour. There is conflicting evidence as to how mobility affects long-term adjustment in children. Where effects have been found, they are often only short-term ones. Other researchers maintain that emotional problems are only aggravated by family moves rather than created specifically by moving. For some, relocation may be an exciting new challenge that stimulates emotional development. For others it can be a temporary, yet serious, set-back.

However, most writers agree on the need for children to be given time to react to the news of an impending move. They should be encouraged to express their feelings, to explore the reasons for the move and the impact it may have on them. Relocation can produce unsettledness and disrupt personal adjustment for a while. However, trying to predict who will experience difficulties and when the effects may manifest themselves is extremely tricky. So many factors can have an influence. The way in which a school handles new arrivals, the pre-move situation of the child, how extensive preparation has been, reasons for the move taking place and the child's situation after the move are all relevant. For this reason, generalizations are best avoided. Each individual case needs to be handled on its own merits.

Educational attainment

Once again, conclusive evidence that changing schools has a direct impact on educational attainment is hard to find. In common with the previous two areas, the problem is one of being able to isolate the effects of a change of school. So many things change when a family relocates, attributing changes in a child to one single cause is extremely difficult. Some educationalists claim that children who move are generally less academically able than their non-mobile counterparts, while others show that there are no differences. Some demonstrate that those who have made several moves are often brighter than their peers because they have had greater opportunities for a wider range of educational experiences.

Where deficits due to moving have been found, they have usually been shown to be only temporary. These deficits can also vary across different subjects. One researcher found that mathematical ability was affected more than reading ability. However, these slight effects were only evident in 7- to 11-year-olds, and not 16-year-olds. The reasons for a child moving were often more influential on academic progress than the move itself.

Conclusions

Evidence from all three areas is clearly inconclusive. It is impossible to state categorically that relocation has ill effects on children, either socially or educationally. However, it would be very unwise to claim that any one child will not experience at least temporary difficulties. Why the confusion? Simply because it is the circumstances surrounding a move that determine the effects of a move rather than the move *per se*.

What can the employer do?

Given the complex nature of the problem, what can employers do to help minimize the impact of educational concerns on parents and children? Experts agree that an individual approach is vital. The context of each relocation, each family, each child needs to be considered on its particular merits. This evidently requires that employers pay careful attention to establishing good communication with employees and their families. In order to understand the context of a move, there must be a willingness to uncover and appreciate any potential difficulties that may arise.

We have highlighted the extent to which relocatees express concern over the effects of a move on their children's education. There is clearly an identifiable need to consider the possibility of providing advisory services to help employees explore the educational options arising from a move. It is likely that such a service would only be taken up by a minority of the total number of relocatees typically moved by an organization. The cost of providing such a service may therefore prove to be less expensive than some organizations may imagine. Cost effectiveness evidently needs to be looked at in the context of total relocation costs, currently estimated to be somewhere between £10 000 and £30 000 per move. Clearly a commitment to reducing the worry associated with relocation must include attention to this emotive issue.

Family and Social Life

As a species, human beings are very much social animals. For most people, having a network of friends is very important. For families who move into a new area, developing friendships is often the first sign of settling in.

Friendship, family and support

Friendships have, not surprisingly, been found to serve very valuable psychological functions. Research shows that people with close friends are much less likely to develop depressive symptoms after experiencing some unpleasant event. This is especially true for women with close friends.

Usually, patterns of friendships tend to change only slowly over time. It is almost as if a slow process of evolution takes place. Gradually we see less of old friends and start to meet new people to whom we gradually become closer. As we change, so our friends change. There are evidently some exceptions, the one or two old friends with whom we never lose contact.

Relocating families face particular difficulties when it comes to this issue of social relationships. The average family in our research sample had moved three times in the previous ten years. Moving every three years or so makes it very difficult for relocating employees and their families to find the kind of support that many of us get from our friends.

It is not surprising to find that having to move away from friends, and in some cases relatives, is a major source of concern for relocating families. On the evidence of our survey, these concerns become more acute once the house move had been completed. What makes this situation particularly difficult is that relocating families are moving away from potential sources of support at a time when they most need them. We asked relocating employees and their partners about the kinds of help, advice and support they had received over the course of their move. Those who said they had received adequate support were significantly less likely to experience stress. As one person put it:

> In a situation like a move, you've got to have someone you can talk to all the time.

Given that relocating families are moving away from their friends, where do they look to for the support they need over this potentially difficult period? Not surprisingly, the answer lies within the family itself. Employees and partners who said that they had a close, confiding marital relationship were much more likely to give a higher rating to the support they had received over the course of their move. Having close friendships outside the marriage was not associated with receiving good support. Indeed, for some partners, mostly women, having a close friend sometimes made the move more difficult. Having to move away from someone you are close to can be very difficult. In some ways the reaction is similar to bereavement. Instead of offering comfort through difficult times, the friendship becomes a source of distress itself.

For employees, mostly men, work colleagues can also be a valuable source of support. However for women in employment, the same does not apply. Exactly why this should be the case is unclear. However, there are several possibilities. Employees are generally changing jobs within the same organization. This may make the transition easier and people in the new office easier to know. There may also be some gender differences in confiding behaviour. Women may find it more satisfying to develop confiding relationships with their partners than with work colleagues. Whatever the interpretation, it appears that partners do not regard work colleagues as a source of support in the way that relocating employees do. However, both employees and their partners appear to be more satisfied with the support they receive if they have a good confiding marital relationship.

The implication is that partners with good confiding marital relationships are better equipped to deal with potential disruption resulting from relocation.

The role of the employer

Given the importance of family relationships in providing mutual support during this potentially difficult time, the aim of those managing relocation should be to keep families together wherever possible. Separating families temporarily during the period between an employee taking up a new post and the family moving house should be avoided. Around half of the families in our research sample reported experiencing such separations. The average length of time spent apart was seventeen weeks. This is one partner's experience of how temporary separation affected her marriage:

> Towards the end of the time we were apart, because the time we had together was so important to both of us, it probably created more stress in our relationship. We tried so hard to avoid having disagreements because the time together was so precious, it actually led to more arguments and disagreements.

Similarly, creating additional workload for employees over the first few months of a new job limits the amount of time a couple can spent together and may inhibit the extent to which they can offer each other mutual support. Around half of all employees surveyed reported an increase in working hours in the first three months of their new job.

The provision of counselling, in the few cases where family difficulties may become extreme, might also prove effective. Although our research suggests that only a very small proportion of relocating families are likely to need such a service, where people feel under great pressure and are unable to talk to anybody, counselling can be very effective. First, it may provide someone sympathetic and supportive to talk to, in confidence, about thoughts and feelings. This kind of help can be useful in cases where either one partner, or both, is moving away from a close friend or relative who has been an important source of support in the past. The following example illustrates the kind of situation under consideration. The person commenting evidently felt very isolated:

> The counsellor knows more about [my difficulties] than my husband. I can't tell him because he's under all this pressure at work as well.

Professional intervention made a difference:

> The counsellor has been marvellous. I hated the company. All they were doing was breaking up families. I really felt I hated them. But I've been able to say how I felt inside to her, and it's really helped enormously.

Second, counselling may also help employees and partners to provide each other with the kind of help and support they need. It is not uncommon for employees to feel guilty about forcing a partner to move in these circumstances. This can sometimes lead to an employee becoming very defensive in the face of their partner's distress. Unfortunately this can sometimes manifest itself as hostility. When a partner feels particularly vulnerable and in need of support, the relocating employee can sometimes interpret this as blaming or pointing the finger. Under these circumstances the marital relationship is not operating at its most effective as a source of mutual support. Counselling can sometimes help to sort these feelings out and restore the marriage to its more usual supportive haven.

Work

Evidence from several researchers suggests that changes brought about at work as a result of relocation do not offer any great difficulties for the majority of employees. Our own work certainly supports this view. From a list of ten potential sources of concern, relocating employees put worries about work firmly at the bottom. When asked about their attitudes and feelings about work, employees showed very little change over the course of the relocation process. Reported job satisfaction, for example, remained relatively constant throughout. This contrasts sharply with reported levels of stress. It appears that although employees do find relocation stressful, changes at work are not the cause.

In light of the fact that around 70% of all relocations involve a promotion of one kind or another, the fact that few employees find changes at work a problem should perhaps come as no surprise. However, a very different picture emerged when partners were asked how they felt about the changes relocation would mean for their work lives.

Contrary to a stereotype popular among many of those responsible for managing relocation, the majority of partners (mostly women) have jobs themselves. Furthermore, most of these women are skilled or professional people, not at all the unskilled part-timers of popular myth. The traditional view of the relocating partner's job as unimportant, unskilled work that pays for the family's little extras is evidently inappropriate. Many partners are actively pursuing their own full-time careers.

When we went back to talk to families six months after moving into their new homes, 48% of partners looking for work had found something. Unfortunately, one in five had had to take a job requiring lower qualifications compared with their old job. Of those who were still looking, 58% were optimistic about finding a new job. These figures mean that around one out of every four relocating partners was still looking for work six months after moving. Half of those were not particularly optimistic about their chances.

That this issue is extremely important is reflected in the fact that a chapter is devoted to it later in the book. Not only do worries about employment and career have a very direct impact on stress among partners, they also rank sixth highest among worries expressed by employees. Given that stress among partners was one of the best predictors of lost work time among relocating employees, partner employment is also an issue of direct relevance to employers.

The implication for relocation policy is that some form of career or employment advice might help partners, and thus families, to adjust successfully to a move. To date, where attempts have been made to provide such a service, they have not been well received. Eighty-seven per cent of partners claiming to have received some kind of assistance in finding a new job reported that assistance to be "not at all helpful". This suggests that partners are not being consulted about the most appropriate kinds of help that they might be offered, and that where help is given its effectiveness is not being assessed.

Summary

Relocating employees and their partners voice concern over different aspects of their moves. Four major issues were identified: property, children, family and social life, and work.

Worries about property are to do with finding a new home, having to sell one house and buy another, and regional differences in house prices. A range of services provided directly by employers, or through a relocation company, are found to be helpful by the majority of those surveyed.

Where families include children, parents worry about the impact of relocation on both their education and social life. However, there is very little conclusive evidence to suggest that moving has lasting effects on children, either socially or educationally. Employers make a valuable contribution through provision of educational counselling for those parents who wish to take advantage of such a service.

Moving away from friends or relatives is something that relocating families often find difficult. Losing a valuable source of support during a potentially demanding period can often be a further source of stress. Families, and in particular the marital relationship, come to represent an important haven for mutual support. Avoiding the separation of families, even temporarily, is a major contribution that employers could make in helping to reduce the potential for relocation difficulties.

Finally, worries about changes in working life are more common among relocating partners. Employees are typically being promoted as part of the move, while partners often find it difficult to maintain forward momentum in their careers. However, employees are aware of the problems facing their partners. Help, in the form of employment advice, was not well received. Wider consultation with partners as to their employment needs should be a feature of relocation packages.

RECOMMENDATIONS FOR HELPING RELOCATING FAMILIES

Improving Relocation Packages

This section looks at what goes to make up a good relocation package as far as employees and their families are concerned. The information has been collected via personal ratings of a wide variety of services that feature in different relocation packages. Each individual service was rated for overall satisfaction, how effectively the company implemented the service, and the extent to which it contributed to a reduction in personal stress. Services associated most strongly with high satisfaction, high effectiveness and low stress are those that deserve greatest attention from the policy makers.

What employees want

The element associated most consistently with ratings of satisfaction, effectiveness and stress concerns *the degree to which relocation packages are tailored to suit individual needs*. If employees believed that their package had been put together in response to their particular situation, they were much happier with the result and much less likely to experience stress. Entirely consistent with this result, the next most important element was provision of relocation counselling. Once again, where employees were happy with this aspect of their package they were happier with the package overall and less likely to report symptoms associated with stress.

Of the remaining package elements, it was satisfaction with the guaranteed price purchase scheme and mortgage subsidies for moving to higher cost areas that was most influential in determining overall impressions of company relocation policy and practice. Although these services are generally well thought of, their significance underscores the importance of monitoring how effectively they are administered.

An interesting picture is emerging as to what improvements might be made to current relocation policy and practice. The importance of tailoring packages individually along with the emphasis given to relocation counselling should be looked at in conjunction with earlier comments. The common themes are *information, communication* and *control*.

Employees, quite naturally, want to know what is happening with their move as it happens. That is only possible if organizations provide relevant information. Employees also want to know that relocation managers are aware of their worries and are prepared to be sufficiently flexible in order to provide effective help. Without adequate communication between these two parties, that cannot possibly be achieved. If these criteria are not met, employees feel as though they lack control over the relocation process, and that can so often provoke stress. These comments from a seasoned relocatee summarize very nicely the spirit of the improvements discussed:

> It's the attitude of people in personnel departments who dictate terms and conditions... thou will, thou shalt... and then proceed to treat applicants like the proverbial bag of potatoes. That doesn't do anything to enhance their reputation or your feelings at the time. It's the attitude of the firm involved towards relocatees: "Are they just a burden on the budget or are they real people who have got real feelings?" It's the little things that count. Advice, help, consideration; anything like that.

What partners want

The pattern of responses among partners is very similar to that discussed above. Overall satisfaction with the relocation package was largely determined by how happy people were with the degree to which it had been tailored to suit their individual needs. The desire for greater flexibility shows in this extract from an interview with a woman who faced some typical difficulties during temporary separation from her husband:

> I don't like the way the company places tight restrictions on things. You get this rather formidable letter that comes, and it says "House Moving", and it lists all kinds of things, like you are allowed this and that. So when you telephone you're always aware that you mustn't talk for too long or it starts coming out of your own pocket. The company don't help by laying all these restrictions down. They don't help.

Quality of relocation counselling also played a large part in the overall assessment of relocation packages.

Partners' assessment of the guaranteed price purchase scheme was an important predictor of overall satisfaction, as it was for employees. Assistance in familiarization with a new area, including provision of pre-move visits, also played a significant part in overall impressions of services provided.

One major difference between partners and employees concerned the importance of satisfaction with short-term accommodation provision. Where partners rated this item helpful, they were much more likely to be satisfied with the package as a whole, be more positive about the extent to which company policy had been effective, and less likely to assess the relocation as stressful. Looking at earlier reactions to the move, this pattern is consistent with the problems partners express when temporarily separated from their spouses. Where organizations provide temporary accommodation for whole families rather than just employees, they are having a direct impact on the degree of stress experienced by spouses, and an indirect, but no less significant, impact on employee stress. This in turn influences attitudes towards the move, the employing organization and their relocation policy.

Summary

This section has concerned ratings of existing relocation policy and practice and what improvements might be made. During the early stages of a move, many employees are not happy with the amount, or timing, of information provided. This, in conjunction with a perceived lack of opportunity to discuss the move with employers, is contributing to stress. The amount of advance notice given was raised. A minimum of eleven weeks was suggested as optimum. Partners were particularly unhappy with the way in which they felt excluded from events. Fifty per cent felt that they were given no opportunity to talk things over with relocation managers. Given the key role played by partners, this was deemed a very serious omission.

Overall ratings of policy and practice made after moving house were generally favourable. Identified weak points were poor information provision and a lack of opportunity to discuss the move with those responsible for managing it. These shortfalls often led to people believing that they had little control over the process. It was noted that poor control is often associated with stress.

More detailed evaluation of relocation packages showed that people were generally very happy with financial services on offer.

However, the more social and advisory elements were perceived as being less helpful. People wanted to see improvements in these services. In particular, employees and partners wanted their relocation packages to be more tailored to suit their individual needs, and wanted more adequate counselling on relocation. Information, communication and control were common themes in comments about improvements.

CONCLUSIONS

The days when employers could deny liability for the effects of their policies on family life are fast disappearing. Work and family life are inextricably bound up together. Many British companies already recognize that fact, and tailor their corporate plans to meet the needs of employees as they arise both at work and at home. Job relocation is an aspect of corporate practice that has a direct impact on the family. It has the potential to create stress for all involved. However, with the benefit of research findings, employees and families can be made aware of the difficulties they may face. Forewarned is forearmed. Expert advice and support can be provided to keep relocation related stress to a minimum, to the mutual benefit of all concerned.

CHAPTER 2 Organizational aspects of job mobility and relocation: a guide for personnel managers

INTRODUCTION

This chapter focuses on the management of job moves from the perspective of organizations, human resource (HR) managers, personnel managers, and employees. For the sake of convenience, job moves are divided into their two component parts. First, the aspect that concerns a change of job, and second the geographical or physical move of home and family. Both are important changes that need to be managed effectively in order to make the relocation a success for employers and employees alike.

Much of the discussion in this chapter is based on the findings of a programme of research, undertaken at the Social and Applied Psychology Unit (SAPU) at the University of Sheffield, which examined the career development, job mobility and relocation of staff in three large British companies. These are well-known companies in the supermarket/retail, electronic/retail, and food manufacturing/retail sectors. For obvious reasons concerning confidentiality, these three organizations are referred to here as Company A, Company B and Company C. Between them, the three employ over 200 000 people of whom some 42 000 are managers or other white-collar professionals. Over 600 relocating staff were involved in three studies from early in 1988 through to the start of 1991. In addition to the questionnaires completed by these people, material from interviews with thirty-five personnel managers and seventy relocating employees will be used to illustrate certain points.

The three companies are very different organizations in terms of their history and development, their corporate plans for the 1990s and their organizational structures and cultures. They do, however, share many similar experiences and problems as far as the management of job change and relocation is concerned.

Organizations commonly instigate a job change or a relocation for an employee in response to one of several demands. For example, another company might have been acquired as the result of a corporate take-over, some restructuring or rationalization may have been undertaken, a new branch or office might have opened, short-term strategic demands such as labour turnover may arise, or a move may simply be the product of a career development strategy. Whatever the reason for a move the issues, facing both the employer, as represented by the HR or personnel department, and the employee, are very similar.

THE MANAGEMENT OF JOB CHANGE

It is clear from interviews with personnel and senior managers in the three companies described above that mobility between jobs is seen as one important way of developing both new recruits and established staff. It enables people to operate in different working environments, and to experience a variety of work groups, managerial styles, and technical systems. Job change is also used as a means of exposing so-called "high-flyers" to radical functional changes as part of accelerated career development programmes.

Relocation is often essential to the effective functioning of many organizations. At the same time, decisions about initiating or accepting company offers of job changes and relocation can be complex for employees. Many different factors have to be taken into consideration. These include consideration of the new job on offer, where the job is based, how the move will influence career development, what the impact of refusing the offer might be, and of course the effect of the move on personal and family circumstances.

In the majority of cases, job change means promotion for an employee. For the employer, however, there are several potential pitfalls associated with the management of these transitions. Research indicates that while many can justifiably claim to "get by", this can often be achieved in a less than effective manner. As a result, considerable strain is imposed on some managers during these transitions. Our research showed that one in seven managers reported generally negative outcomes to their last job change.

In all three of the companies we looked at, several aspects of the management of these transitions gave cause for concern. The first of these concerns is to do with the reasons companies give for wanting to move employees between jobs. Over half of all the job changes we surveyed were initiated by the employer.

It was quite clear from our results that employers and employees can have very different views about job moves. As noted above, employers can use them primarily as a means of filling vacated posts caused by labour turnover, to compensate for poor succession planning, to smooth the path of rationalization or corporate acquisitions, as a reward in the form of a promotion and, lastly, as a career development tool. Employees view job moves as being almost entirely a career step. However, moves which are necessary for the effective functioning of the organization are not always good career steps for employees. It should, therefore, come as no surprise that job changes may not always have the positive outcomes anticipated by either companies or their employees. This quote from a senior personnel manager in Company A, which expanded both in terms of market share and numbers of employees during the 1980s:

> We have over-promoted people. There is no doubt about that. We have put people into positions which they should never have been put into and which they haven't been trained for. That is generally in new stores but I know it happens elsewhere. We fall into the trap of expecting too much from people and then we end up disciplining them because they are not doing the job properly—the reality is that we often don't give people the right kind of support and training to do the job in the first place.

A second concern is the small number of women who are relocating with their jobs. Women represented only 11% of the total number of employees changing jobs during the research. In general, the women in these surveys did not believe that there was genuine equality of opportunity for mobility and promotion within their companies.

It is clear that talented and motivated women increasingly resent being treated as potentially less mobile by their organizations simply by virtue of their gender. If this situation persists women may become more reluctant in the future to join organizations where career advancement depends on mobility. One effect already being felt is growth in the numbers of women who are turning their backs on large companies in preference to self-employment.

The third concern is to do with the amount of prior notice people are given of an impending job change. Around 30% of all those questioned were given less than two weeks' notice prior to starting new jobs. Only 13% had more than two months' notice. Analyses clearly show that the longer the period of notice given to employees, the more likely they were to settle quickly into new job roles and to report positive outcomes to job changes. This no doubt has something to do with the fact that it becomes easier for employees to wind up their old job, and prepare adequately for the change and the challenges of their new job. This process of disengagement, and the impact it can have on employees, is something often overlooked by organizations. Also, advance notice helps employees to maintain a sense of direction, autonomy and control over these transitions. Organizational research has consistently demonstrated that adequate preparation and feelings of control are important factors in facilitating successful changes at work.

The fourth concern relates to the support available to people in new jobs. Almost all of these managers and professionals exhibited a strong sense of self-efficacy and self-esteem and felt able to perform well in new situations. However, over 60% said that they would have benefited from greater support from their immediate superior and colleagues during this settling in period. Over 50% reported a need for the provision of clearer job descriptions and clearer work guide-lines during this period. Over 60% reported feelings of isolation, uncertainties about new work roles, a lack of influence in their new jobs and problems created by changes of managerial styles.

There was a consistent degree of dissatisfaction with the interpersonal support available in new job situations, particularly with the induction and training procedures which accompanied functional job changes. Significantly, one in five managers in the interview group felt that their performance appraisals following their last job move had suffered to some extent. As an example, consider these comments from a senior personnel manager in Company C:

> We actually have what we consider to be a good induction and training programme for those moving into new jobs. The problems arise when we have to move someone quickly and all that careful planning just goes out of the window. Another problem is that whilst we are trying to get line-managers to be more responsible for developing their junior people some just pay lip service to this and of course *their* performance appraisals are all about bottom-line things like profitability and costs. So, some don't think that it's worth their while wasting time, as they see it, and so some job changes are not as well managed as we would like them to be.

In spite of these difficulties, it must be emphasized that, given time, most staff do settle down to new job roles. However, given the expected need for greater staff flexibility and mobility in the 1990s, these generally *laissez-faire* policies may become increasingly ineffective. These concerns were articulated by many of the personnel managers we interviewed. They expressed reservations about the ways that their companies managed employee job changes. All felt that more resources, human and financial, should be invested in these areas.

The attitude of some senior managers towards people coming into new jobs was frequently described as "sink or swim". This may well reflect the existence of an "I made it the hard way so they can too" attitude which is still prevalent in some companies. While stressing general improvements in human resource management during the 1980s, most of the personnel managers we spoke to felt that much remains to be done in the future to ease adaptation to these transitions.

A typical example of the kinds of difficulties that employees can face during job changes is captured in these extracts from an interview with a senior manager who has worked for his company for seven years:

> Experiencing job changes with [name of company] is like driving in fog—you're often not sure where you are or where you're going. The last job change I had was certainly the most difficult—I had very little notice and because it involved a functional move at the company's request, I was expecting to get training on the job. As it turned out I didn't get any, which was exactly what had happened with other job changes so I suppose I shouldn't have been surprised. Well, to cut a long story short, I found myself in real difficulties because the job I was doing was very different and I couldn't seem to get anyone to understand the problems I was having.

> I think that my performance appraisal certainly suffered this year as a consequence. But, as I said earlier, the only thing this company is interested in is how you perform in a job—even if they drop you right in it.

To conclude, while most of these men and women did settle down in their new job roles, many expressed dissatisfaction with the preparation and briefing they received prior to the job change, the job descriptions they received and the management of their transitions into new posts. What steps companies can take to manage these transitions more effectively is discussed below (see p. 45).

RELOCATION MANAGEMENT

The general view of employers in these surveys is that the management of the personal side of job moves is the responsibility of the individual employee. Typically, the relocation support they provided was aimed specifically at the (usually male) employee and covered the financial aspects of moves such as help with mortgage differentials, providing disturbance allowances and so on. Where the companies did recognize employees' personal circumstances (e.g. spouses' employment status or the potential effects of relocation on employees' families), this was always dealt with on an informal and *ad hoc* basis.

This, and other research studies show that while personnel managers may be sensitive to the problems of relocating staff, directors and senior managers often appear to be unaware of the potentially disruptive effects of a move on employees and their dependants. Very few organizations have any formal policies on helping relocatees with either lengthy or highly stressful and problematic moves.

The following quote, from an interview with a senior personnel manager in Company A, illustrates the kind of worries personnel managers can have:

> The first thing to say is that mobility is essential if you want to get on in [name of company]. I wouldn't say that we were "dead-end" people who do not want to move—but it is bound to slow them down. But, we use people like draught pieces at times—moving them here there and everywhere at the drop of a hat.

> The problem is that the company says that if an employee moves—whether it's good or bad for them—the relocation is their problem. We'll help with the financial side but everything else is up to them. This may have done in the past but it simply won't do now. I can see the stresses and strains increasing all the time.

> Our managers work very hard and having to work sixty hours a week whilst trying to buy and sell houses, get your kids into new schools, being separated from your family, spouses having to give up jobs to move and so on, is putting intolerable strains on some of our people. What I don't know is how we can assess what this is doing to our staff and what we can do about it.

As with research reported in Chapter 1, a majority of relocating employees in the three organizations surveyed gave positive ratings to the often generous financial support they received during relocations. However, they were concerned about the lack of support in other areas.

People were typically worried about potential disruption to family life, settling into a new job, disruption to children's education, separation from family, commuting long distances and so forth. Stress is evidently more likely when several problems and difficulties arise during moves.

One important factor associated with stress was the length of time it took for people to complete the relocation process. The process begins with receiving notice of the impending move, and ends with settling into permanent accommodation in the new area. The longer this period, the more likely people were to experience stress.

Reported stress among dual career couples was higher than among families with one principal salary earner. Difficulties with finding suitable employment after a move was a common problem for relocating partners.

There are, not surprisingly, variations across the three organizations, but the results clearly show that stress attributable to relocation is not necessarily associated with single factors like buying and selling houses. Elements from both work and personal life can cause problems. The findings have important implications for adjustments to the kind of relocation support currently provided by companies.

What might these problems be costing companies in financial terms? Although it is extremely difficult to provide precise figures, we can make some rough estimates.

The average cost of a relocation varies between £10 000 and £30 000 per employee (Shortland, 1990). These costs will increase for each month that an employee is trying to settle into the new area (for example, living in hotels). One-quarter of relocating staff reported that relocation had a markedly negative effect on their work performance. If we assume that an employee is working as little as 10% under par over a six-month period and earns a salary of £25 000 a year, even this limited reduction in work performance may be costing an employer £1250. If a company is relocating 400 staff a year and one-quarter of them experience these problems, the direct cost will be around £125 000 a year in terms of reduced work performance.

In our estimation, these are extremely conservative figures. They take no account of the potential costs to these organizations of staff taking time off work to deal with relocation related problems, lengthy and expensive stays in hotels, poorer performance appraisals following job changes and the effects on people's personal lives.

Problematic job moves can also engender negative attitudes among staff towards their companies and towards future relocations. The data show that moves that had a disruptive effect on spouses and children led, at least in the short term, to an increased reluctance to relocate. Where staff are asked to accept job transfers for reasons of succession planning, refusal rates can have serious implications for companies.

Many interviewees recalled the difficulties which they and their families had encountered while relocating. This section concludes with extracts from two interviews with relocatees. Their experiences mirror those of many of their peers:

> Financially, you have to say that it is a good package—the complaints that I have are to do with all the other things that you associate with relocation like buying and selling the house and uprooting your family. I was separated from the wife and kids for six months and I think that the problems we all encountered certainly had an effect on my work.... My wife found the whole thing very stressful, having to deal with potential buyers. And when she did move she felt very isolated, and then we had some difficulties finding suitable schools for the kids. She also had to give up her job which turned out to be a serious loss for us. It took her a long time to find a suitable job. But, I know that the company doesn't care about all this as long as you are doing a good job for them during the week.

> (Senior manager aged 36. Eight years' service. Partner in full-time paid employment. Two children aged eight and eleven)

> Well, relocation is just bloody awful whichever way you look at it. We had all the usual hassles with estate agents and solicitor's incompetence and were badly let down by potential buyers. The upshot of all this was that it was ten months after I actually started the job that we actually moved into our new house and it looks like we'll be moving again next year.... It was even more stressful for my wife as she had to leave her family and had a lot of friends in the North. Because of the hours I was working she felt very isolated and it took her a long time to get out and make new friends—and that was through a colleague's wife. Luckily, the children were too young to notice but I can see problems when they get older.

> (Manager aged 28 with five years' service. Partner not in paid employment. Two children aged five and two)

PROBLEMS FACED BY PERSONNEL MANAGERS

Surveys of these three organizations suggest that relocation is not only a problem for employees and their families. Some personnel managers experience difficulties in managing job mobility. In interviews, "fire-fighting" and "crisis management" were commonly used phrases when talking about the management of job change and relocation. There was also a widespread belief that personnel functions do not have the resources, human or financial, to provide more help with employee mobility. Why does this situation exist? As long ago as 1978, Legge made these observations about resourcing tasks in personnel management:

> ...to obtain resources to undertake these tasks, a personnel department requires power which, at present, in many organisations it lacks, precisely because of its inability to convince those who do control resources of its potential contribution. It is the old chicken and egg situation. Until personnel can demonstrate its contribution to organisational success, it will be unable to generate adequate resources for its work, but until it does so, it will be unable to achieve this potential contribution.

These comments apply equally well to the status of personnel functions in the 1990s. Rather than having the resources to plan for and anticipate potential difficulties, those working in personnel can only hope to react swiftly and effectively to problems already identified. This certainly applies to relocation and the level of support provided for relocating employees. The situation owes much to the attitudes of senior managers working outside of personnel functions. It is a commonly held belief that assisting with the personal side of relocation is not company business and represents an unwarranted intrusion into the private lives of employees. The following quote is from a senior executive in Company B:

> I'm not saying that refusing moves would blot a person's copybook, but you know when you join [the company] that at times you have to be mobile to get on, and that obviously can involve some sacrifices in your personal life. But, we have to take the view that if an employee goes for a relocation then that's their decision. ... I think it would be intolerable to start meddling in people's private lives—I mean, where would it end? These are issues which our staff have to

talk through at home—if they don't want to move then that's their business. ... I believe that the relocation package which we provide is very competitive and generous and I don't see how we could justify doing any more.

However, as the research evidence demonstrates so clearly, views such as those expressed above run counter to the experiences of those directly responsible for managing relocation, who voice frustration at being unable to provide more support for employees. One of the most consistent complaints from relocatees was the lack of personal support provided by their companies during their moves.

The severity of difficulties experienced by some people has led, at least in the short term, to an increased reluctance to relocate. This may have important implications for both individual career prospects and for an organization's ability to fill new and vacated posts and manage succession planning systems. These findings should be a cause for concern for all companies where mobility is an integral feature of organizational life.

GOOD PRACTICE

What makes this particular research programme unique is the opportunity it has given to both employees and personnel managers to voice their opinions concerning steps that organizations might take to manage relocation more effectively. This section looks at a number of specific policy recommendations based on the comments of those taking part in the research.

Of course one always hopes that recommendations about company policy and practice will be taken on board by those concerned. However, in the case of relocation, there is a danger that policy changes will be applied in a general way with little regard for the individual needs of employees and their families. Perhaps the most important point arising from this research is the commonly expressed sentiment that relocation management be responsive to the unique circumstances surrounding each individual move. Providing "off-the-peg" packages that take no account of the novel circumstances facing each employee, each family, is often the cause of major difficulties. We have been surprised to find that relocation doesn't appear to get any easier the more times it is experienced. Our interviewees have told us that this is simply because each move is different. Circumstances change: children get older, partners get different jobs, the housing market alters. This comment is from a seasoned relocatee:

> You always worry about a move. Having made mistakes before, you worry that you might be making mistakes again. You just don't know until you've been there for six months.

Mobility management needs to be flexible, take account of changing individual career goals and personal circumstances, and regularly updated in response to changing corporate goals and human resource management policies.

Company policy on relocation will naturally need to reflect the circumstances of both the organization and its market. Important factors will include size of the company, its geographical distribution, and the frequency of job changes or relocations employees expect. Even more fundamental to effective mobility management are the availability of financial, technical and human resources to personnel departments, and the degree of power and influence they wield within the organization.

With these considerations in mind, the following suggestions are offered as the basis of a guide to good practice in the management of job changes and relocation.

Managing Job Changes

1. Job changes can obviously benefit employees. Given time, most will adjust successfully to the demands of new jobs, even where transitions are extremely difficult. However, there is a widespread feeling among the men and women in these surveys that the management of these transitions is often left too much to chance. In particular, care needs to be taken to ensure that the best person is always chosen for the job. In the jargon of the

management consultants, the aim is to see that an optimum person/job fit results. The sign of a well managed job change is an employee who adapts quickly and painlessly to the demands of a new job. Care needs to be taken that should problems of adjustment arise, there are mechanisms in place that enable senior managers to identify the difficulty promptly. Having recognized the problem, there needs to be swift and adequate provision of technical training and personal support that can help the employee through any temporary predicament.

2. A review of the interviewing procedures that currently accompany job changes may be a worthwhile exercise. Recruitment professionals continue to be critical of the ways that many British companies handle employee selection procedures. Organizations might benefit from consulting specialists with demonstrated expertise in this field to review current practices, and advise personnel officers and line managers as to recent advances in the field.

3. A substantial number of the employees we surveyed expressed serious doubts as to whether there was genuine equality of opportunity within their organizations. Several believed that they had only limited control over opportunities for career advancement, further training, and geographical mobility. Informal and subjective systems of monitoring and assessing management performance are common in many organizations. Along with informal appraisal processes, patronage is seemingly inevitable in any hierarchy, whether it be commercial, political or academic. However, it is important that these informal systems are kept in check by more objective methods of assessment. Subjective nepotism, while inevitable, needs to be handled responsibly. This is essential if people are to believe that their employers reward, in a fair manner, good performance and the overall contribution which the employee makes to the organization.

4. Job transfers initiated by organizations should be based on encouragement rather than coercion. While essential to the effective functioning of many organizations at the present time (particularly those with labour turnover problems), they can

often be unpopular types of moves for employees. With this fact in mind, there should always be open and honest communication about what the benefits and pitfalls are for employees who are being encouraged to move by their employers.

5. Improvements in the management of job change are likely to be most effective when planned systematically rather than implemented in response to short-term manpower demands. Ideally, every job change should be accompanied by a realistic consideration of how it will figure in the overall requirements of the organization, and equally important, in the career goals of the employee.

6. Coping with change is made considerably easier when extensive and reliable information about new circumstances is provided. Similarly, the longer that people have to assimilate that information, the more likely they are to find the change, when it does come, easier to handle. Organizations should aim to give employees as much notice as possible of impending job changes. Similarly, staff should be given accurate and realistic job previews prior to moves. There was widespread dissatisfaction, in these companies, with the quality of literature accompanying a change of job. Accurate job descriptions and other relevant information should be made available to employees well in advance of any impending move.

7. Taking responsibility for the well-being of people in new jobs is no easy task. Newcomers in the survey reported an enormous degree of variety in the quality and quantity of help they received in the early stages from their line managers. Speedy and successful adjustment is important to both the employee and the organization. Consideration should be given to the provision, for managers responsible for this supervisory function, of specialist training in the skills that such roles demand.

8. The induction and training procedures which accompany radical job changes often warrant examination in many organizations. Where a job change involves a marked shift in function for the employee, adaptation can be difficult, not least because the change often represents a critical career move. People making moves of this kind deserve to be monitored closely.

One suggestion for making the process of adaptation to radical change run smoothly was to establish hand-over periods with the previous job holder. Typically, a period of at least a week was thought to be desirable.

9. Early performance reviews which follow a job change often need to be handled with care. It is all too easy to attribute the conduct of a new incumbent to individual failings rather than problems arising from a transfer. Work overload, protracted transfer procedures, and ineffective induction can all have dramatic, but temporary, effects on performance. The more radical the change, the more likely these difficulties are. Responding by initiating yet another change will often serve only to provide another good manager with an impossible task to fulfil. The potential drain on resources that this process might lead to is self-evident.

10. Both this research project and others like it have shown that male employees are far more likely to be offered a relocation than their female colleagues. Married women in particular experience discrimination when it comes to consideration of their potential for mobility. Many more women will be entering professional career streams in the 1990s. The traditional family with a single male breadwinner is in the minority. Employers are increasingly faced with the challenge of not only attracting talented women employees, but also enabling them to develop their careers through mobility where it is necessary.

Managing Relocation

1. A clear message has come from relocating employees, their families, and those responsible for managing their moves. Relocation can, and often is, a difficult process. Organizations responsible for initiating these moves need to be aware of the potential problems faced by all those concerned. One place to start is by compiling and maintaining a "mobility audit". This is simply a body of information that can be used to identify the kind of difficulties relocating employees and their families experience, and the most effective form in which support might be offered.

2. People are concerned that reporting relocation-related prob-
    lems to their employers may have some adverse effect on their
    career development. Organizations should seek to allay these
    concerns. It is in the best interests of employers and employees
    alike that a relocation progresses as smoothly as possible.
    Identifying potential difficulties as and when they arise is
    essential to this process. People should be encouraged to main-
    tain an active dialogue with those responsible for managing a
    move.

3. Wherever possible, two months' notice should be given prior
    to any impending relocation. Where families are involved, par-
    ticular attention to this period of notice is desirable. Successful
    adjustment depends on adequate preparation. The longer
    employees have to prepare for a move, the more effective their
    preparation. Adequate advance notice also helps the employee
    and his or her family maintain a sense of control over events.
    Research has consistently demonstrated that feelings of control
    are an important buffer against the potentially negative impact
    of events like relocation.

4. The fate of relocation "refusniks" was another common source
    of concern for employees. There was a distinct impression, valid
    or otherwise, that refusal to accept a relocation, once offered,
    would result in career development grinding to a premature
    halt. Organizations operating such a policy would be guilty of
    wasting valuable management resources. There are very often
    good personal reasons as to why an employee would seek to
    postpone a move. Typical examples include clashes with a
    child's educational milestone, such as GCSE examination
    courses, or required time for a partner to organize a job trans-
    fer. Many of those employees who turn down a move may be
    very willing to reconsider in six months' or one year's time.
    Sensitivity to the timing of a relocation is important.

5. As with other research that has given employees the opportunity
    to voice their opinions concerning relocation management, our
    results suggest that a more individual and personalized
    approach would be welcomed by many. However, it is equally
    true to say that some people would consider more personal

approaches to their moves as an unwarranted intrusion into their private lives. For that reason, the extent to which individual needs are discussed and catered for should be tailored to suit each employee. As already noted, the temptation to construct "off-the-peg" packages that offer all things to all families should be avoided. Some people will doubtless prefer to get on with it by themselves once financial supports have been negotiated. For others, involving the whole family in discussions about relocation is an effective way of creating a caring and attentive climate right at the start of the process.

6. Living in temporary accommodation, particularly when it means being separated from one's family, is strongly associated with relocation-related stress. Wherever possible, organizations should ensure that families have the option of staying together during a move. Where the local housing market permits it, some organizations provide temporary accommodation for the whole family rather than pay hotel bills and travelling expenses for the individual employee. This has the potential to reduce the stresses caused by separation, and gives partners more time and opportunities to find jobs, locate suitable schools for the children, get to know the area, and find suitable housing.

7. For many people, relocation can be a lengthy business. Slumps in the housing market can lead to problems with selling, while booms can create difficulties for buyers. Either way, it is not uncommon for the relocation process to last for several months, if not over a year. Evidently, the longer the process goes on, the more stressful it becomes. Keeping a close watch on those involved in more protracted moves is often an effective way of pre-empting difficulties, or at least being able to deal with them quickly and effectively.

8. Organizations may need to cast a more critical eye over services provided to their staff by solicitors and estate agents. Over 70% of the managers in these surveys expressed concern about the quality of property services provided. Buying and selling one's home is a stressful experience at the best of times. Where professional services are perceived to be inadequate, the problems are magnified. From an employer's point of view,

the most carefully planned relocation packages can be sabo-
taged by the unthinking actions of a third party. Given the
extent to which their employees provide custom for solicitors
and estate agents, many organizations are in a position to
lobby for improved customer services.

9. In many organizations it is common for relocation manage-
    ment to be taken on by people in personnel departments, often
    in addition to other responsibilities. However, where the vol-
    ume of relocations within a single organization merits it, a more
    viable alternative might be to create a new post of Mobility and
    Relocation Manager. This co-ordinating post would comple-
    ment and lend support to existing personnel functions (partic-
    ularly Remunerations and Benefits). Such a manager would
    need to have experience in several areas of personnel manage-
    ment, including training, career development, succession plan-
    ning, job changes and relocation. This person might also have
    some experience in counselling work. The cost of creating this
    post would represent a tiny fraction of the relocation budgets
    of most large companies. Alternatively, where the number of
    employees relocated is considerably smaller, organizations
    might benefit from employing qualified consultants, with
    demonstrated expertise in relocation, to monitor mobility and
    relocation management on an ongoing basis.

10. There are obstacles to successful relocation management that
    need to be tackled at a national level. In spite of recent changes
    in the rules governing conveyancing procedures, the process of
    house buying and selling is unlikely to get any easier in the
    short term. Large organizations with a vested interest in reloca-
    tion, perhaps in conjunction with the CBI's Employee Relocation
    Council, should consider putting pressure on legislators to
    reform house conveyancing procedures. They continue to be a
    major impediment to smooth mobility at the present time.

11. Organizations may need to co-operate with each other to estab-
    lish spouse-employment information networks and support
    services along the lines of those that have existed in the USA
    for some time. Initiatives of this sort are likely to come from
    board-level, perhaps in conjunction with other organizations
    such as the CBI.

CONCLUSION: WHERE DO COMPANIES GO FROM HERE?

As is often the case with recommendations concerning a single issue such as relocation, too few human resource specialists and personnel managers have the time to study them in detail. When generated from research findings, they are too often dismissed as the machinations of a detached "expert". In this case it may be worth bearing in mind that the points covered in the previous sections were raised by a large and diverse group of managers and professionals. The recommendations listed were developed from many conversations with employees and relocation professionals talking openly and honestly about their experiences, good and bad, of job changes and relocations.

This chapter has provided an overview of the problems of relocation as viewed by employees and relocation managers. Most organizational and labour-market analysts anticipate that the domestic and international labour markets of the third millennium will demand greater flexibility and mobility from employees. Many British companies are already facing greater competition in the recruitment of graduates and professional staff from foreign companies based in continental Europe. Furthermore, it is anticipated that there will be one-third fewer young people entering the labour markets of the mid-1990s. Lastly, increasing numbers of young women and men are seeking careers and employment packages which take account of their whole lifestyle—occupational, familial and personal. Hence, those companies that have a proven track record in people-centred human resource management, including mobility management, are likely to enjoy a head start over their competitors in staff recruitment and retention in the 1990s and beyond.

CHAPTER 3   Women and relocation

INTRODUCTION

> Although many organisations do an excellent job of handling the physical logistics of the move, few facilitate the spouse's creation of a meaningful life…. Creating a meaningful portable life is one of the areas in which much can be done to improve the expatriate assignment from the perspective of the spouse, the employee and the company.
>
> (Adler, 1991, p. 275)

> Life on the international circuit is just a big black plastic sack—you throw everything into it when you move, hoping you'll have time to sort it out at the next house, or the one after that. I've a loft full of them now…. I sit there with all those packages and wonder what shall I do with my life?
>
> (Foreign Service wife)

This chapter discusses the professional and personal issues surrounding the relocation of women. Consideration will be given to the problems faced by employers, personnel managers and their female staff. Suggestions will also be made concerning a range of initiatives for organizations, personnel and human resource executives and individual transferring partners. These ideas are based on the author's involvement, over many years, with working women at various career levels and stages. The comments and experiences of many highly mobile women are interspersed throughout the chapter. Many of these come from unsolicited letters, others are portions of confidential interviews, workshops, discussions, career counselling sessions and unpublished project work.

THE TRAILING SPOUSE

The issues surrounding the female "trailing spouse" are complex. From an organizational perspective, the questions to be addressed include: is a "trailing spouse" really the company's responsibility or not? How much does she (or he) affect relocation success and employee performance? To what extent is business success dependent upon them? Furthermore, with the expansion of transnational business comes a need for an internationally mobile work-force as well as increased domestic relocation. Another important factor is the changing role of women. Demographic changes and skills shortages are further considerations.

Spouse dissatisfaction has been an important factor in resistance to relocation, particularly over the last ten years. However, it is only recently that British companies have begun to acknowledge this fact. American researchers have observed how male attitudes to relocation have changed from unthinking acceptance of the corporation's values to the selection of jobs according to personal lifestyle. Recent British surveys of spouses/partners on international and domestic assignments, have shown that many employees believe that having working spouses and partners can inhibit international mobility and that employers were aware of this resistance. Yet, most British employers still maintain that the personal side of relocation is essentially the concern of the employee, focusing their relocation support on the financial aspects of the move.

In Britain, increasing numbers of women, single or married, have entered the labour market over recent years, and this trend is set to continue. Women now account for around 44% of the labour force. More than half of all households now have two wage-earners. Fewer than a third of employed husbands now have economically inactive wives. In the United States, the Department of Commerce projects that 80% of families will be dual-earner by the year 2000. A Maternity Rights report showed that nearly half of all mothers return to work within nine months of having a baby. They are also more likely to go back to full-time work in the same job with the same employer compared with a decade ago. There now remains only a small percentage of traditional families with a single male breadwinner and stay-at-home spouse.

Styles of partnership have also changed in recent years. Alongside conventional marriages, where married women now combine work and family responsibilities, there are growing numbers of dual career couples. Other variations on the traditional family type can also be found, such as: long-term stable relationships outside of marriage, relationships in which women are the main family breadwinners, and single-parent business women. As more women are being sent abroad as part of their own career development, roles within families become reversed. The problem male partner is becoming a more common relocation phenomenon.

The numbers of working women in the international business community are unlikely to decline. As the supply of young people eligible for employment slows down, so the demand for women to enter the jobs market will increase. By 1993, there will be one million fewer 16–19-year-olds than a decade earlier. This coincides with growth in the number of jobs available. Over the next five years, it is estimated that the numbers of women in paid employment will increase by 10%. This compares with a 4% increase in the numbers of men at work. Employment opportunities for the five million women aged between 16 and 60 who do not work are greater than ever, and women are responding positively.

At the same time, international trade is expanding. The European Economic Community, Eastern Europe, and the Pacific Basin are just three areas offering growth to eager multinational organizations. A recent United Nations survey of world-wide trends reported that one-quarter of all goods and services on the world market originate from large multinational corporations. As these organizations bid to capture an ever larger share of the world market, so it becomes more common to find experienced employees being relocated from one country to another.

Many internationally mobile employees have partners who are increasingly unwilling to trail meekly behind. Relocation presents women with a special challenge: it takes a toll of professional and personal effectiveness, promotion opportunities, support networks, financial independence. They face language difficulties, enforced idleness and disruption to their lives and career plans. For many, relocation means dislocation:

> I sometimes think I must be the world's greatest living expert on relocation as I am currently moving into my 26th home in 29 years of (yes!) happy marriage. Many of these homes were in the 12 years when my husband was a mining engineer in Malaysia. He became the trouble-shooter and we were moved, sometimes at three monthly intervals, between the company's 15 mines, in addition to coming home either every two or three years for six months and renting another house (and packing up the previous one entirely)....
> My private formula is a good howl, dust myself off and set about finding something to do quickly before you go mad. So far it's worked!

There are, of course, some women who are content with old style, expatriate traditions and performing supportive social and welfare roles.

> We were obedient—we weren't like today's young women. We just went where we were told, and at times we actually enjoyed it… but now, when I think back, we only enjoyed it because we didn't realize there was any other choice. My daughters are different… they say "no".

However, personnel and Human Resource (HR) managers should not assume it is an acceptable lifestyle for everyone. New arrivals often welcome help in a new community, but they resent social patronage, cattiness and claustrophobic attitudes. For women accustomed to full-time careers, enforced career breaks can be frustrating, isolating and demoralizing experiences. Few British companies give any formal help to the partners of relocating employees. Instead, most continue to handle the problem on a case-by-case, *ad hoc* basis.

The financial implications of an unsuccessful relocation cannot be overstated: the price of an international assignment package may amount to four times an employee's annual salary. A recent estimate of domestic relocation costs suggests transfer budgets as high as £57 880 per employee. In times of economic downturn, the retention of key staff is priceless. If, as surveys show, spouse resistance to relocation is a major obstacle to mobility, then *ad hoc*, eleventh hour assistance is insufficient. Spouse dissatisfaction may prove to be very expensive indeed.

What can be done to help spouses adapt to a new environment and have a meaningful portable life? In the following sections two important themes are examined: first, organizational initiatives, and second, the promotion of self-help by women themselves. The emphasis is on practical measures, particularly for dealing with the most difficult situation of all: when a career spouse is barred from continuing employment because of local employment restrictions. These policy recommendations are applicable in both domestic and international contexts. A short, third, section is devoted to the special needs of single businesswomen and women who are primary wage earners.

ORGANIZATIONAL INITIATIVES

> I sit there for hours, listening to them talking on and on about the relocation policy, but when I ask "What does your wife think about the move?" there is complete silence. They have no idea. They're much too busy worrying about which shipper to hire.

> (relocation consultant)

Often the working spouse is the last person to hear about the decision to relocate. The employee is usually the sole focus of the company's attention and is depended upon to communicate all the details of the transfer arrangement to spouse and family. But modern couples, particularly dual income pairs, have to merge their working and family lives, plan by consensus and negotiate career priorities jointly. When a well-qualified, highly professional woman receives second-hand information and pressure to conform to corporate orders, relocation resistance and refusal is more likely to follow.

There are some hopeful signs that corporations are beginning to offer a more sophisticated approach to relocation with projects such as the spouse employment seminar organized on behalf of BP's Engineering Division in November 1990. However, the pace of change is very slow and the small offerings which are available appear to be *ad hoc* improvisations rather than well thought out, long-term policy strategies. Consultants suggest personal assistance be given only if resistance to relocation is experienced, while overseas information services continue to report being over-whelmed with cries for help from relocation personnel who do not know what to do with "difficult" working spouses.

Working Spouses

Perhaps the greatest worry of many relocation specialists is the negative attitudes which many managers, including personnel managers, have towards dual career couples. A senior HR man-ager (female) reported:

> The MD said "I don't want any of these working married couples— they are far too much trouble".

It would appear that corporate relocation policy is often dictated by insensitivity rather than intentional discrimination. Because most relocatees were male breadwinners in the past, it is all too easy to assume present-day transferees will be the same. In fact, many women perceive themselves as having careers rather than jobs, and are committed to a range of partnership arrangements, from traditional marriages to stable relationships outside of mar-riage. Relocation management companies also report an increasing number of single female transferees, and even a few trailing hus-bands. As one researcher notes:

> A generation ago professional women would abandon their careers if their husband had to relocate. Today, it may be the husband who relocates if his wife gets a "too-good-to-pass-up" offer in a distant city.

Thus the working spouse, whether male or female, with or without a marriage certificate, is now an established part of the two-income unit. Job mobility and relocation can cause particular problems for these couples.

Corporations should be aware that relocating spouses do not expect companies to guarantee jobs, make personal decisions or undertake complete responsibility for every aspect of a transfer. What is needed, however, is reasonable and appropriate attention to the reality of the situation facing working spouses. If relocation failures are to be avoided, if retaining key personnel is a top priority, if retaining the competitive edge in recruitment is prized, then improved assistance for the working spouses must be addressed.

There are various kinds of help companies can offer relocating women in order to make a transfer as attractive as possible.

Involvement of Partners

Women say they want to be involved in all relocation issues from the start. As partners of employees, they want to feel the company cares about their well-being. They look for direct communication with relocation personnel, before, during and after the move. When organizations, for various reasons, are unable or unwilling to involve the accompanying spouse from the earliest possible stage, female resentment and suspicion is very likely to grow. Transfer arrangements may then become jeopardized.

Many employers believe the main reason for partner relocation resistance is financial, the loss of a second income. But survey results suggest this may not be the only factor. In a recent survey, 40% of respondents agreed that damage to partners' careers and consequent loss of partners' career progression/opportunity are major reasons for a refusal to relocate. The authors comment that

> ...even though the international assignment offered to their husband is financially attractive, it does not compensate for the loss of control that comes from giving up a well paid job or career and relying on someone else financially.

Many women who have been involved with the Career Development Centre for Women in a professional capacity are reluctant to voice worries about their partner's careers, fearing that this will damage promotion prospects. When an invitation arrives to come along to the office "for a chat" with an unknown authority figure, spouses are likely to be inhibited and restrained—even more so if children are also expected to attend. A preferable option might be to invite partners along to other events in the annual corporate hospitality programme. Group events, such as a spouse social or seminar, in a pleasant relaxed atmosphere away from the firm's premises, may provide a more attractive setting. Employee get-togethers could be used for airing spouse concerns. Informal discussion groups are cheap and simple to set up and provide useful opportunities for relocation and other personnel to attend on a supportive and non-participating basis. This would enable companies to project a more caring image and enable personnel managers to obtain valuable information and feedback from their employees' partners.

Companies sometimes complain that trailing wives do not respond to their spouse support initiatives. Often, however, women know nothing about them. The information simply does not reach them. It is not unknown for management to voice reluctance about contacting the family directly, on the grounds that it may cause embarrassment should an employee's partner not be their legal spouse. Some employees even tell their partners not to use spouse assistance if they have to request it. It seems pointless to set up elaborate fact-finding questionnaires or offer invitations to partner events if the relocating employee completes the form-filling or refuses to convey invitations. More worrying are the attitudes of male managers in companies, as this article in *Personnel Management* observed:

> Many senior managers outside personnel felt that assisting with the personal side of relocation represented an unwarranted intrusion into the private lives of employees. This view runs counter to beliefs expressed both by relocating staff and those directly responsible for managing relocation.

> (Forster and Munton, 1991)

It is also insensitive for an immaculately turned-out young female personnel officer to arrive on the doorstep of a harassed working wife and mother to persuade her of the joys of moving to the Third World. A more useful approach would be to involve expatriate spouses with their experience and understanding of family relocation concerns. They could also act as mentors and provide feedback about in-country opportunities, and offer contacts for settling-in support. Equal opportunity departments, which are now part of many transnational corporations, should be able to provide the necessary training in women's career relocation.

Many employees have never heard of the term "spouse assistance" and have no idea support might exist or what it entails. In-house newsletters, journals and employee handbooks could remedy this by highlighting such details. Whatever the difficulties involved, two-way communication between the company and the mobile spouse is essential.

Choice

Instead of imposing mobility upon employees, an effective step is to offer employees long periods of notice prior to transfers. Transfers should also be based on encouragement rather than coercion as there may be good personal reasons why an employee initially refuses to move. For example, Marks & Spencer plc move their managers from store to store as part of their career development. They aim to have staff operating efficiently and speedily in their new location. About five years ago, their domestic transfer policy changed from the "stick principle", whereby management decided who was moved and where, to individual choice. Now all management vacancies are advertised and managers themselves decide whether to apply or not. By offering choice in relocation decisions, this company has reduced the "hassle factor" of relocation resistance and introduced a welcome family orientation into transfer decisions.

Ideally, organizations should offer induction programmes for the whole family during the pre-departure stage. When providing help to trailing spouses, a range of support, financial and otherwise, is usually appreciated. Although language training and work permit help (for overseas assignments) is sometimes offered, it is rare to hear of compensation for childcare and lost income during pre-assignment activities (reconnaissance visits, house hunting, reviewing schools, etc.). Many organizations offer courses and briefings on practical matters such as climate, culture and creepy-crawlies, but this is inadequate in terms of orientation for the working wife.

Employment

It is very important to cater for the individual needs of mobile women because a relocating woman may be one or several of the following: a full-time mother of a young family; full-time mother of school-age children; mother of teenagers; mother of independent young adults; a free-lance consultant; working full-time; working part-time; half of a dual career couple; looking to return to work; taking a career break; a highly qualified professional; half of a stable, but unmarried, partnership; working by choice; working to balance the family budget; working for a rival company; working for the same company; a single parent; a single business woman or solely responsible for elderly parents.

Relocating women are not all the same. Companies who are open-minded and flexible enough to realize and apply this knowledge will score over those who don't.

Very few companies keep records of whether the spouses of employees work or not, or spouse CVs. When obtaining such data, personnel should make the purpose clear to both employee and spouse, and provide essential assurances about confidentiality. If and when a relocation occurs, regularly updated mobility audits can provide a helpful base from which companies may offer and fine tune appropriate spouse employment assistance.

Spouse employment assistance should aim to provide a flexible package to help the spouse of an employee find satisfactory employment in the new location. It may include career counselling, life planning, self-marketing and job application techniques. In-company expertise in personnel or human resource departments may already exist to some extent, but a professional from Catalyst, the US national resource organization, warns:

> ...one standard [spouse employment assistance] package will not be effective in addressing all employees' needs.

Spouse employment assistance should include a range of services from which the accompanying partner may chose appropriate elements depending on individual needs and transfer location. Some specialist women's career consultancies may have "portable careers" services designed for relocating women which can be bought in on a case-by-case basis or formatted to group workshop needs.

An important component in career counselling for relocating women is a thorough analysis of skills they have acquired from all aspects of their experience—paid employment as well as unpaid work in the home, neighbourhood and community—which can be transferred from one area of life (and location) to another. The career consultant should be thoroughly familiar with the life/work planning techniques and have a full grasp of volunteer opportunities, distance learning packages, re-entry strategies, career-break updating and network contacts. Spouse programmes offered by non-specialists or relocation consultants should be thoroughly checked: one rather vague sounding "expert" turned out to be a mental illness practitioner! Programmes imported from abroad which rely heavily on techniques such as unfamiliar self-assessment exercises, are often unhelpful.

It is insufficient to offer, for example, a Teaching English as a Foreign Language (TEFL) course to every woman regardless of her interests and abilities. In economic downturns, organizations may be reluctant to invest in a wide range of spouse facilities, but most of the following provisions do not require huge financial resources. Many may already exist in equal opportunity, human resource and training departments. Some are tried and tested, others are just useful suggestions.

Examples of these are:

- Corporate data-banks for inventories about job openings, education and re-training opportunities in various locations.
- Corporate links with other firms in the new location.
- Office facilities made available to spouses seeking work.
- Liaison with other companies already at the transfer location for job opportunities and support information.
- Advertisements in commercial and in-house magazines for dual career postings and spouse profiles.
- For both employees and spouses: flexible patterns of work (job-sharing, part-time, short-term assignments, telecommuting, consultancy, etc.) in the new location.
- Career counselling for the relocating couple and the family as a unit.

Wider Family Responsibilities

Considerable anxiety surrounds many middle-stage families with responsibility for ageing and dependent family members. As average life expectancy lengthens there are increasing numbers of older people and a move abroad for several years may cause anxieties and concerns. Organizations should be aware of these potential worries for employees and consider introducing home leave provision and holiday visits for dependent relatives as well as school children in the relocation package.

> We've been posted to the Far East for three years... maybe four. Father died a while ago, so mother is on her own now, and I'm an only child. I'm really afraid I won't ever see her again.
>
> (oil wife)

Single Business Women

For business women on their own, an active parent in an accompanying role is an invaluable, yet often forgotten, resource for whom the relocation policy may be adapted.

> Every time I move I say I'll never do it again, but one forgets. As a female on my own, there are so many practical things to do which I can never manage alone. The house I live in now needed painting but I didn't know the neighbours yet, so there was no one to leave a key with. I don't know how I would have managed without Mum.
>
> (senior personnel manager)

When employers consider potential relocatees, they often overlook the single business woman. Women's national and international career development lags well behind that of their male colleagues. If they are mono-track careerists within the company's employ, they expect equal opportunities for mobility regardless of marital status. Corporate policy needs to be reconsidered in light of the changes in women's economic activity. There are three main areas of concern. First, companies must change chauvinistic attitudes which assume that women are afraid to relocate or lack the personal attributes necessary to cope with foreign assignments. There are still assumptions that all women are really looking for is marriage-and-a-family, so they will not have a long-term career commitment—and certainly not one which includes working abroad.

Second, perceptions concerning the attitudes of foreigners towards professional women are often based more on racial stereotypes than fact, as this women manager observed:

> I'd love to work abroad for a year or two, so I asked about the possibility of an overseas transfer during my annual appraisal. He said no, because the only opportunities were likely to be in Hong Kong and, according to him, the culture was against women there.

(senior fund manager)

Many of the more liberal European countries have women in practically every industry and at all levels of management. In Pacific locations, a person is seen as a foreigner first rather than a man or woman. As one observer commented:

> Companies should realize that foreigners do not treat expatriate women in the same ways that they treat their local women.

Middle Eastern and Latin American companies believe only the best representatives will be sent out to them. Consequently if the best person happens to be a business woman, she will be treated particularly well.

A third concern is the belief that the international business game is too difficult for women to master. The concern seems misplaced. Many professional women hold graduate degrees, such as MBAs, are fluent in several languages, and possess excellent social skills. Where women are seen to underachieve, companies might consider that an alternative explanation may be that other male expatriates find working with women managers, particularly as superiors, extremely difficult.

The Trailing Husband

Where a woman is the main family wage earner and is singled out for relocation, the difficulty of the trailing husband is raised. Married women are just as interested in mobility as married men, but decision-makers worry that their husbands will probably refuse to follow them. The key difference is that a senior, fast-track woman transferee is more likely to consult her spouse prior to relocation agreement rather than a male counterpart.

As yet, there are only a small number of trailing husbands but employers should be aware that there will be an increasing number of these in the future. As more women achieve promotion, so the numbers of male "trailers" are likely to rise. Companies who tackle this issue early on will greatly advantage themselves.

Short- and Medium-Term Support

> I arrived in England alone with two babies and all the baggage. We're exhausted and cold after a very long-haul journey. I'm not British, knew no one, it was all completely unfamiliar. There wasn't anyone to meet me and not even a car had been arranged to take us to the hotel.
>
> (oil company wife, PhD)

Women come very quickly into direct contact with the realities of a new location. Whether a woman is working or not, she will be responsible for many of the practical and emotional adjustments in the new home and community. Corporate assistance, therefore, should concentrate on ensuring short-term needs are properly covered: "comfort assistance" (accommodation, warmth, food, transport) and practical help (shopping, medical provision, baby-sitters, and so on).

For working spouses, the demands are even more onerous. Not only does she have to settle into her new job, often immediately after arrival in a new area, but she also has to take on lifestyle concerns as well. Business women, with or without partners, usually have to rely exclusively on themselves. House-hunting and home-making is often limited to evenings and weekends. Some say resident company wives make matters worse by looking after "helpless" bachelors but ignoring working partners or single women. Here, adjustments to the relocation timetable could be made to provide extra settling-in time for employees.

Even after a few months in a new location, many women can still experience isolation and loneliness. For women previously in employment, but now forced to discontinue their careers, it can become a structureless role full of boredom, frustration and, eventually, resentment. Changes in organizational policy might include:

- In-country support and follow-up by appropriate staff with international experience.
- Covering the fees for professional memberships, conferences and seminars.
- Subscriptions to cover the costs of "keep-in-touch schemes".
- Up-dating course on return home.
- Contact with and sponsorship of international resource services.
- A strict limit on employee travel during the early months in the new location.

Returning Home

On returning home after an overseas assignment, many partners find that their mobile lifestyle has created a fragmented and incoherent CV. One women commented:

> My spouse's work has been a major obstacle in all my job applications. I have good qualifications, useful both here and overseas, but as soon as I reach the interview stage and they see all the overseas postings, my application is dismissed.

> (Foreign Service wife)

Organizations can assist the job-search of re-entry spouses in several ways. Volunteer work is devalued and dismissed by many recruiters as irrelevant to commercial skills. The skills acquired in the non-paid sector by many relocated spouses is thought to be completely different to those learned in the High Street. This assumption should be questioned. Employers may be depriving themselves of hard-working, dedicated people whose job experience is unusual but whose skills are honed sharp.

Staff selection executives may also like to rethink their response to CV formats. Most are familiar with a chronological-type presentation, wherein applicants list educational and work history from school-days onwards. Such formats seriously disadvantage many women. They emphasize career gaps and contain out-of-date information. Organizations, especially those who complain they can never find "suitable" staff, could advantage themselves by becoming more open-minded to various job application styles and may avoid rejecting potential employees just because they do not follow familiar career pathways.

Conclusion

The majority of today's professional business women have a strong commitment to continuous employment in their careers. However, relocation will always have the potential to disrupt this. The transfer of a family is likely to include a working spouse with expectations and a voice of her own. To exclude her needs from transfer negotiations is not only inequitable; it can damage organizational performance and the company's image.

No one is suggesting organizations must offer guarantees or become gurus on every course, country or career. But if the spouse—as many indicate—is such a valuable contributor to successful employee transfer, recognition of her uniquely difficult challenge requires increased company responsibility as a feature of normal transfer practice.

SELF-HELP FOR RELOCATING WOMEN

These are some of the questions which relocating women, whether employed or not, are likely to ask:

- How can I maintain or enhance job-related skills?
- How can I have a progressive career if I move so often?
- What can I do with myself all the time if I can't get a work permit?
- What is the value of the international experience I've had?
- I'm sick of just being a useful pair of hands. … I want a special niche of my own. How can I "belong" somewhere?

- I've nothing to show for all the years of travelling
- How do I job-hunt in a foreign country?
- What about *my* career prospects?

Many react with despair on hearing the news about a move. At first, the choices seem clear cut: either you say goodbye to a career and go along with the arrangements, reluctantly, disagreeably or resentfully, or you dig in your heels and flatly refuse to move. Whichever path you take appears completely unsatisfactory. You feel as if your needs are unimportant, your employment valueless and your worries irrelevant. "Loyal" wives, after all, do not rock the marital boat, block his promotion prospects or abandon attractive husbands to foreign shores for years at a time—alone.

What other choices do you have? What can you do to help yourself create a meaningful role and a purposeful portable life? First of all, recognize the relocation stress and deal with it early on. Experts suggest moving is traumatic when it involves a change of "life area"—job, family, neighbours, leisure interests. Side-step thoughtless remarks such as "What did she expect if she married someone in a job like that? Surely she must have known...". Sharing your feelings with others who have been through similar processes is often very reassuring, as you soon realize your reactions are not especially unique. Women's support groups, especially those with mobility experience, are good sources of help and referral.

Next—DON'T PANIC! Just for the moment, take time to calm down and think matters through—there are probably far more choices available than you think. Refusing to relocate or becoming an unwilling "trailing spouse" are just two extreme strategies. Rather than see it as a collision course, a better tactic is to make the relocation work positively for you. The most successful women on overseas postings are those who can self-activate, think creatively and grasp opportunities. Many mobile women find work everywhere they want to without extra qualifications or extensive retraining. They know their skills, strengths and resources, they research a range of employment openings and learn how to match their talents to the available opportunities. Instead of looking for just one type of job, they close no doors until they have thoroughly examined every possibility.

In 1982, a group of volunteer American wives on overseas posting to the UK founded the FOCUS Information Service. FOCUS began in a small way, with little money and voluntary helpers in a borrowed basement. Now they have an impressive list of sponsors and a thriving membership. FOCUS provides a wide range of services: expatriate information, advice, guidance, courses, newsletter, liaison with other countries, networking, job opportunities. The friendly staff are still mainly volunteers, women who return home with up-to-date CVs plus concrete, marketable international experience—and their relocation has been fun and fruitful.

Employment problems for a spouse are just one of the many considerations to be discussed prior to relocation. As a working woman, mobility can incur major career disadvantages—perhaps more than a baby-break. But, it is essential to be aware of the limits to company assistance. For example, the couple themselves must decide whose career has present priority. Evidently jobs cannot be guaranteed world-wide.

Spouse employment assistance is rarely formalized, but this does not necessarily mean it does not exist. Some companies respond on a case-by-case basis, so you should not hesitate to ask for assistance—and, should it be unavailable, enquire about other sources of help. Do remember, though, at the end of the day, final decisions about the future are your responsibility.

This section continues with some practical steps, beginning with pre-departure. Then there are ideas for maintaining career relevance during the relocation, whether or not you are employed. Next, preparation for home re-entry, and, finally material for single business women and those who are primary wage earners.

Before You Go

The two most important things a relocated woman needs before the transfer actually takes place are *information* and *contacts*.

Information

Information most valuable at this stage comes under three headings:

- Information about the decision to relocate.
- Information about the new location (physical character-istics, social amenities and employment opportunities).
- Information about yourself, i.e. your transferable skills, career goals, life plans.

Information about the decision to relocate. It is very tempting to com-plain about the people or company in charge of relocation to any available ear. While it may make you feel better, it often achieves nothing constructive. A more useful approach is to use your energy to discover as much as possible about the new assignment details.

If the transfer decision has not yet been finalized, find out who is discussing what with whom, when the matter is likely to be decided and who you can talk to about it. Some are reluctant to face bosses or relocation managers with these sorts of questions. If so, remember this: as an accompanying spouse, *you* are the key person in relocation, the one who can make or break settling-in time, job performance, corporate image, etc., and, above all, the company's financial investment. The organization wants to con-vince *you* that the relocation will succeed but cannot do so if you are invisible or silent.

If you are invited to the office—with or without children—for a "chat" about relocation and hesitate to accept, ask for an alterna-tive venue. Make it clear you welcome the opportunity to meet. Suggest a time and place in which you feel comfortable. Enquire if other spouses will be present and ask if a group meeting is planned as well.

Information about the new location. You need to know everything about the physical, social and employment details in the new loca-tion. It is essential to prepare for overseas assignments with knowl-edge about health, climate, safety, language, culture, society, etc., by attending briefing courses and orientation programmes.

Information about your employment prospects is also necessary. It is vital that the job search starts before you leave home. Take advantage of meetings, seminars, briefings, personnel, data-banks, professional memberships, journals and so on to discover all and any prospects in the new location. Learn how to market yourself effectively, noting forms of CV, résumé, etc. for various countries. Companies may be able to offer some or all of the following:

- Spouse employment assistance.
- Career counselling.
- CV preparation.
- Job-search techniques.
- Access to job banks.
- Payment for training/courses.
- Language training.
- Small business training.
- Office facilities (stationery, postage, telephone calls, facsimile machines, photocopying, word processing).
- Spouse workshops; spouse seminars.

More information about employment in the new location may be available from:

- Relocation consultants.
- Resource service such as FOCUS, London.
- Women's professional/business networks.
- Host country embassy/Chambers of Commerce.
- Charity directories.
- International voluntary organizations.
- Books on international job-hunting.

Information about yourself. Pre-departure information is incomplete without taking stock of your resources and planning goals for the future. Whether you are employed or not, the stock-taking process identifies strengths, clarifies priorities and puts you on track to consider a range of new options. You can make an *informed* decision about your future. Thinking in terms of "once a teacher, always a teacher" limits the full range of employment options. A teacher, for example, has special subject knowledge plus transferable skills:

team-work, writing, budgeting, counselling, liaison, organizing, public speaking. Look for help with the assessment stage from the following sources.

● *Local Adult Education or Community Colleges.* Women's short courses are designed to help update women's skills and often include down-to-earth, practical exercises and ideas for taking stock. One of the biggest advantages of these courses is sharing with other students, which boosts confidence, experiences and new ideas. The Women Returners Network and Working Mothers Association (WMA Returner's Pack is useful) may also be able to help you find a suitable local course or group.

● *Self-assessment books.* The *Springboard Women's Development Book* by Willis and Daisley is specially designed for women. Others, like *What Color is Your Parachute?* by Bolles, is the US best-seller for job-hunters. Try the local library careers section, careers services and quality booksellers.

● *Local Careers Service.* Aimed mostly at young people, some also advise adults. Their large information resources should be open to anyone, but always ask if other facilities exist. Be sensitive to the times when the service is crowded with young school leavers.

● *Fee charging career services.* Most provide a mix of tests, questionnaires and self-assessment exercises, some of which can only be used by qualified psychologists, to evaluate your potential. Some also offer personal development counselling or practical help with job hunting, CV preparation, interview skills, time management. Look for those who specialize in women, relocation, skills analysis and career/life planning techniques.

Contacts

Contacts are required to keep in touch with home and create links in the new location. The power and influence of the male "old-boy" networks has given rise to many women's information, advice and support groups. These networks may be informal groups, where members share a common interest, or more formal associations for professionals.

Relocation incurs the loss of many important links with business contacts. Networking memberships brings many benefits, including keeping in touch with current developments, job information, journals and people, at home and in the new location. Contacts also maintain your visibility while you are away.

Contacts from business/professional world. The European Women's Management Development Network brings together EEC women managers; the UK Federation of Business and Professional Women has an international network and there are many specialized women's networks (e.g. Women in Banking, Engineering, Management, Publishing) whose activities may be world-wide. (See Selected Further Information, p. 161.)

Other places where contacts can be made. In the UK, there are partners groups for the foreign service, armed forces, British Council (here, it is a "wives and husbands" group) and other military personnel. There are information and resource centres, such as FOCUS in London. Many national associations have an international membership, including the Women's Institute, National Women's (formerly "Housewives") Register, National Childbirth Trust, etc. Also:

- Religious organizations.
- University, polytechnic, community college, school associations.
- Voluntary organizations.
- Sports, crafts, arts, etc. groups.

Maintaining Career Relevance During Relocation

The choices for working women during relocation include:

- Continuing paid employment.
- Taking time out/baby-break.
- Free-lance/self-employment.

- Becoming a commuter couple.
- Telecommuting.
- Part-time and other flexible patterns of work.
- Non-paid work.

If you are unable to work

If you are unable to take up any paid employment in the new location, plan to use the time fruitfully. Career counselling and action planning at the pre-departure stage will help identify meaningful goals to attain and avoid the depressing and demotivating drift. A period overseas as a dependent spouse is often perceived as a disadvantage and, certainly, re-rooting in the new community is demanding. But, there are also opportunities for developing unsung skills and talents.

Look to your personal development. Is it time to learn something new? What gaps exist in your employment experience? Can you acquire them in the voluntary sector? Can you help others by sharing existing skills? Do you have latent talents just waiting to be discovered?

Find out what activities exist in your host environment, which international or local volunteer groups relate to your new country and details of available distance or "open" learning schemes. Join informal and international networks, programmes initiated by other wives and corporate, government, community projects. Grasp unpaid opportunities within the expatriate community, offer a "home-country" flavoured service, become foreign correspondent for your home-town newspaper/professional journal/in-house magazine, write reports, give talks. Travel, as they say, broadens the mind. So does continuing education, increasing self-awareness, getting physically fit, enjoying and valuing the family.

If you can work, but not in your chosen field

If you have an established career already when transfer occurs but cannot work as you wish, consider adding a new dimension to your skills portfolio. Possibilities will exist to acquire specialist skills and consolidate undeveloped ones. For example:

- Local ethnic expertise.
- International corporate practices.
- People skills: public speaking, negotiating, interviewing.
- Group skills: chairing meetings, delegating, decision making.
- Foreign currency knowledge.
- Foreign exchange know-how.
- Local communication/marketing.
- Local economic trends, sales techniques.
- Enhance/update your self-marketing.

Adjusting to work

Once relocated, you will need to adapt to both a new office and a new home. Four suggestions for the adjustment stage at work:

1. Expect your level of performance to be low at first, and your efficiency. Even after 6 months on the job, your performance may be only 50–70% as high as it used to be. Know that reduced job performance is normal.
2. Expect to be exhausted. When everything is new, just coping with routine matters can demand an enormous amount of energy. Establish some of your favourite routines—sport, cinema, foods. The more familiar your activities the easier your adjustment will be.
3. Expect to be stressed. Keep in touch with former friends and colleagues as it will take time to make friends in the new place.
4. Count on a let-down when you least expect it. After the rush of activity in the first few weeks, you may suffer a let-down as you realize everything you have lost. Be patient with yourself.

Some communities have organized ways of welcoming newcomers, but most lack such facilities. Newcomers, fending for themselves, must earn acceptance in the host community. At first, it is best not to seem too different. Be respectful of other expatriates and their way of living, interested and helpful, although you may not agree with their values and lifestyle. Once you are an accepted part of the community you are in a better position to make choices, pass opinions and suggest changes.

Self-employment and free-lancing

Of all the options open to a relocating spouse, the most portable and attractive is self-employment. The advantages include independence, variety, freedom from commuting. On the down side, there is the high rate of small business failures, long hours, financial insecurity, lack of help and interruptions. If you are seriously interested in self-employment, your first investment should be one of the many small business courses before leaving home.

Free-lancing your professional skills and services to a variety of clients on short-term contract or consultancy basis is another attractive option. With this option, you gain a level of security and income without losing time and location flexibility. As with self-employment, there are all the advantages of flexibility and independence, but pitfalls as well. Have you good credentials? Have you got what it takes to keep the work coming in? Take a course, talk to others in the field and read about it first.

Preparing for employment on returning home

Most experts suggest returning home should be treated in exactly the same way as any other relocation. Follow, then, the pre-departure information and contact paragraphs at the start of this section. In addition, obtain as good a picture as possible about the job market from reports in business magazines and newspapers. Employment fields change over time, some expanding, others going into decline. Look at current job advertisements, not merely to see their relevance to you, but also to familiarize yourself with present-day employer needs. Consider retraining and professional updating for out-of-touch skills: contact networking groups for details.

High-mobility and fragmented employment does not create a good impression on job application forms or CVs for prospective employers. Relocated women's CVs fail for two main reasons: they use out-of-date CV formats and they include too much detailed information. Consult a career counsellor (maybe the one you saw prior to departure) for help in creating a fresh CV or obtain one of the many excellent books available.

Single Business Women

At present, relatively few international managers are women and they are most likely to be the first female managers to be sent abroad by their company. If you are planning a long-term world-wide career, the process is probably one of mutual education: encouraging companies to experiment while increasing their confidence in your professional permanence and seriousness.

Pre-departure planning should include a realistic timetable for relocation. Couples often split domestic and office tasks between them. Solos have but one pair of hands—for packing up, finding a home, settling in and sorting out. An interesting idea suggested by one senior business woman was to include a widowed parent in the transfer arrangements. In her case, mother acted as "wife" and dealt with the household matters. Other items to consider for inclusion in your relocation agreement are: home-visit frequency and fares for holiday visits to you by parents and siblings.

Personal security during the journey and in the new location should have a high priority. It makes good sense to shun accommodation in darkly-lit hotel rooms on ground floors and to avoid airlines treating business women travellers as secretaries or "companions". The Business Women's Travel Club offers helpful advice and recommendations. Upon arrival, view areas with good street lighting, integral car parking, nearby public transport, sensible locks and neighbours. Ask real-estate consultants to recommend reliable decorators, electricians, etc. and enquire about local cultural customs, no-go areas and for help-line telephone numbers.

Assumptions about swinging singles sometimes cause social misunderstandings with expatriate families. A solo business women has fewer opportunities to meet the resident community and local club membership may be restricted to males only. It is helpful to get to know one family really well, keep in close touch with family and friends at home and follow local cultural guide-lines. If you travel frequently, it may be difficult to maintain a close personal relationship, or even begin one.

In the new office, keep a low profile at the start. Make non-committed contacts, find out about the office pecking order and keep a paint-on smile on your face, regardless. Take plenty of time to find out how best to blend in with everyone else, especially if you are "trail-blazing" as the company's pioneer female executive. Your "honeymoon" period will soon be over, so use it wisely while it lasts.

Trailing Husbands

At the moment, there are relatively few examples of trailing husbands alongside relocated business women. But numbers can only increase and the transfer process will again challenge traditional assumptions.

International female transferees usually insist upon agreeing arrangements for the trailing menfolk before an assignment decision is agreed. These partners may be already in occupations which transfer easily. Others must go where facilities exist for them to carry on working. For example, academics may be able to arrange a sabbatical or be keen to take post-graduate courses.

The relocation package will, of course, include all the usual features such as home leave and matters pertaining to children, if appropriate. But, some say transfer policies offer a better deal to mobile men than to women, so it may be wise to check details carefully, as this quote from a senior personnel manager illustrates:

> I applied for the job in February. Nine months later, it still had not been filled. I'd been offered it several times, but I refused because, firstly there was no increase in salary, and also it meant my partner had to give up his job. I suggested the company rented a flat for me in the new place. Then either I could stay there during the week whilst he continued working from home, or we both moved in but didn't sell our place—we'd let it instead to cover his lost income. They said no. Eventually, they brought in a man whose experience is far less than mine, got him a smart well-decorated place in a better area, whilst his wife carried on her business from home.
>
> (senior personnel manager)

Consider also inviting corporate contributions to cover visits to and from older parents for whom you are responsible. "Eldercare" as the Americans call it, is a growing demand on women, particularly those in mid-life, and neither you nor they should be deprived of ongoing attention, contact or crisis assistance if you are far away.

Before departure, the joint demands of home responsibilities and work demands can be highly stressful. It is essential to delegate as many tasks as possible. If you find it hard to ask for help, are on 24-hour call and over-committed, you lose control and endanger everyone who depends on you. Structure and manage your time schedule, including an allowance for personal relaxation. Put a limit on exquisitely performed chores, say "no" to time robbers (interruptions, drop-in-for-coffees, salespeople, uninvited visitors) and allow even the youngest to do their bit. Even amateur help is better than nothing if it saves you time.

In the new location, insist on sufficient time for attending to dependants' needs to avoid trouble later. With children, your role will change to that of a busy, working mother-cum-tourist-guide during holiday visits. Perhaps a term-time only arrangement can be negotiated or an agreed shorter hours schedule for holiday periods. When children must stay at home while you travel, quality childcare and reliable back-up provisions are essential.

Menfolk may not have foreseen the extent of disruption to their lives created by the relocation and now find themselves in the novel situation as "dependant". To gain the support you need during an adjustment period, it may be wise to expect an unsettled stage. Give your relationship special attention.

CONCLUSIONS: WOMEN ON THE MOVE

> In an international move, the spouse has the most difficult role of any family member.
>
> (Adler, 1991, p. 257)

The preceding sections have concentrated on practical aspects of relocating spouses but, in the longer term, important questions remain to be addressed by mobile couples and organizations alike.

Among them is a major issue: whose responsibility is it to assist spouses, the employee's or the organization's?

As matters stand at the moment, there is considerable confusion. Organizations, for the most part, believe the limit of their responsibility is the provision of financial and housing related support to the main breadwinner.

Spouses believe that employers are generally insensitive to their needs, at upper management level. They feel "knee-jerk" solutions are ineffective, inflexible and out of touch with the reality of relocation in the 1990s. Employment-orientated women are in the majority, they suggest, yet relocation packages often seem to be more concerned with administrative convenience for personnel managers rather than a service for the people being moved.

It seems clear that successful relocation management policies involve both work and non-work domains and neither organizations nor transferring women can wait for the other party to solve their difficulties. Companies can play a more influential role in negotiating bilateral agreements in foreign countries, thus allowing incoming spouses to by-pass normal work permit legislation. They can also increase their awareness of the changing role of women, heighten partnerships with community organizations and spouse service organizations and, above all, communicate their concern in human relocation factors in concrete and tangible ways to reduce misunderstandings and accusations of disinterest.

Meanwhile, spouses may wish to re-examine their own response to relocation and adopt a more pro-active stance both as individuals and through various women's groups and networks. An excellent example of this is WICE, a French non-profit educational and cultural institute, who set up an international event *Women on the Move*. The two-day conference, in Paris in 1990, attracted over 350 delegates from sixteen countries. The conference emphasized the need for spouse services and greater attention to the complexity of the lives of women "on the move". Similar conferences are planned for the future and may provide a strong platform for change.

Organizations say they are sometimes given the impression that families expect them to become corporate nursemaids for all aspects of relocation. This is not so. Foremost is the urgent need for international employers to acknowledge the reality of dual career couples with an increased attention to the needs of spouses. This is not a "soft" issue; it makes hard financial sense for organizations to become people-centred as the quality of home life affects the employee's ability to perform at work. If organizations wish to retain key personnel and reduce unsuccessful transfers, they must commit themselves to providing relocation packages which take account of the needs of professional women.

CHAPTER 4 Corporate relocations: a jigsaw puzzle in human resource management

INTRODUCTION

If one were to give a synopsis of company relocations from an interested bystander's point of view, one might say that corporate relocations are one of those rare organizational events where management is leading (though more often than not, unintentionally) the organization into a crisis. Yet somehow, most of those concerned emerge from a relocation unscarred.

It is a *crisis* because so many things can, and do, go wrong throughout the life course of a relocation. Even if everything went entirely satisfactorily, according to plan, it could be potentially a crisis for some. It is an *unintentional* crisis because management does not expect it to be one, which could only make things worse.

However, the vast majority of individuals concerned come out of this lengthy, complicated and often agonizing process, unharmed. Contrary to what might be expected from a series of "mini traumas"—selling a house, looking for a house, buying a house; looking for a job for the spouse; looking for a school for the children; moving; cutting off relationships with friends; making new acquaintances; closing up an office; moving into a new and different one; most probably changing some aspects of one's job—in spite of all that, most people, most of the time, cope very well.

CORPORATE RELOCATIONS IN THE CONTEXT OF ORGANIZATIONAL CHANGE

Before taking you, step by step, through the key phases of a typical relocation, a comment about relocation as a special case of organizational change is called for.

A Corporate Relocation is an Optional Change which Needs Explaining

Organizational changes typically occur as a result of induced events, i.e. because something happens that forces a change in the "normal" routine of an organization. It could be a personal change—the chairman, chief executive or some other key figure ceases to function (moves to a new job/resigns/is fired/falls ill/dies) or changes in the market and business environment dictate corresponding organizational change (contraction/expansion of certain functions). These changes *legitimize* the corresponding organizational changes. They tend to be viewed as *force majeure* which in some way facilitates their acceptance.

Not so with corporate relocations. These, although often driven by *force majeure* (end of lease, contraction/expansion of business) are less acceptable, because while the *reason* for relocation could be clear cut, the *choice* of relocation, is not. There are numerous options (combination of locations, size/type of premises, relocation times). Relocation, rightly or wrongly, is seen by many as an *optional* change. While people can be convinced by the necessity of relocation, they tend to believe that the options chosen require some explanation. A failure to do so convincingly, may put the whole process on the wrong footing. The first signs of trouble are when the grapevine communicates that the chosen location is next to the chairman's golf course!

A Corporate Relocation is an All-Encompassing Change Process

A corporate relocation can be described as a hub of change of different kinds and magnitudes. First, there is the office relocation itself. This is the narrowest aspect of relocation, and one which is fully attended to by companies: a company will move your desk and other work artefacts as a matter of course. This by itself, though simple, may have some far-reaching implications because of the *symbolic* overtones present in a work environment, which we would normally take for granted, until such time when the environment in its entirety changes (a discussion on the role of symbols and how to manage them comes later).

Then, we have two typical changes associated with a company's relocation. First, there are some structural changes: there is almost always some qualitative change in the work organization. It is quite common to take the opportunity of a corporate relocation to affect an organizational change (see Relocation and Reorganization, p. 109); but that apart, the new offices will rarely have the same *spatial* arrangement as before and that alone would affect communication patterns.

Second, there are non-work changes which affect the relocatee and his or her kin—a topic elaborated elsewhere in this book. Here company policies differ. While some will assume responsibility for some of the upheaval of a familial relocation (help in finding the spouse work and help in finding a school for the children are the most common), others will limit their assistance to the direct technical aspects of relocation (a house search and perhaps a mortgage assistance scheme). In other words, the typical company takes a limited view of its responsibilities as the instigator of change. This typical attitude has two principal implications: first, an explicit expectation for a swift relocation and a "business as usual a.s.a.p." approach; and second, an implicit assumption separating work issues from non-work concerns. While the first may be seen as legitimate concerns and allowed to surface (e.g. lack of public transport to and from work), the latter are not. Any pressures, difficulties, or dissatisfactions to do with the wider manifestations of relocation (e.g. children unhappy at school) are considered to be the employee's private affairs which are best left to the individual concerned to sort out.

A Corporate Relocation is Calling for Leadership

What we have said so far is that a corporate relocation, more often than not, will be viewed as an *optional* change that needs explaining;

more often than not, it will create a major upheaval in the relocatee's life. This unleashes some of the less pleasant aspects of change
processes: uncertainty, ambiguity, doubts, questions, resentment,
anxieties. For these reasons, a relocation calls for *leadership* which
will instil confidence, that:

- Someone is in charge.
- The person(s) in charge know what they are doing.

In practice that would call for a clear message, providing a con-
vincing case for the relocation and for the specifics of the choice;
issued by the most senior position in the organization and communicated *directly* to all concerned, preferably in a specially convened
meeting (a common device is also a video-taped address by the
Chief Executive Officer, distributed to all employees concerned).
But this approach has to be sustained throughout the period of
relocation, by frequent updates, unambiguous information, and
ongoing visible backing from the most senior positions.

A Corporate Relocation Requires Three Different Leadership Roles

While the Chief Executive Officer needs to be visible at various
points throughout the relocation period, the day-to-day management of the relocation process requires three distinct leadership
roles, representing the three main areas of change (see Figure 4.1).

- First, a *Project Manager*, who will look after the relocation
  of business (the core, but narrow constituent of the
  change). This requires project management skills, good
  planning, proficiency in technical detail, task orientation
  and a great deal of leg work.
- Second, a *Public Relations Person* who is good at communicating, who can enhance the positive aspects of the
  venture and play down the negative; the sort of person
  who has a ready answer to an unexpected question, in
  short: this task calls for a *sales* approach—someone who
  can "sell" the project to concerned stakeholders: first and
  foremost to relocatees, but also to other significant parties:
  clients, suppliers and significant internals.

PR/salesman

Work issues
(general)

Ambiguity, uncertainty
doubts, concerns,
resentment

Reassurance and persuasion

Empathy and helping skills

Task orientation and technical competence

Work and non-work
issues (personal)

Career/life goals,
family concerns,
private information

Relocation issues
(technical)

When – how – where – what

People person   Project manager

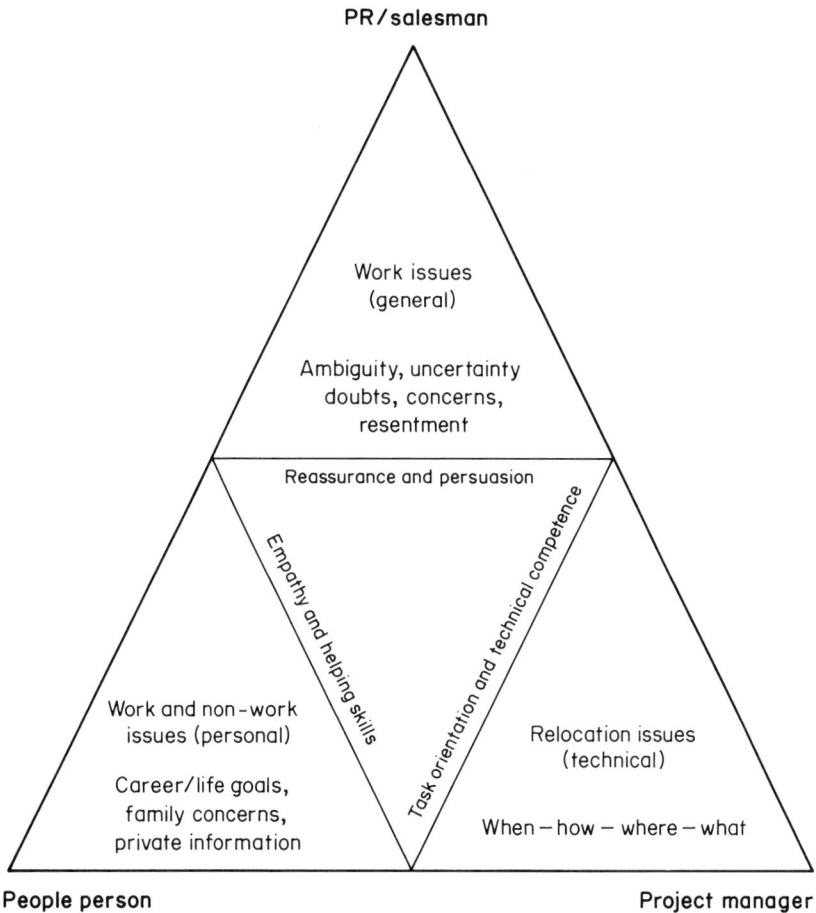

Figure 4.1   The three roles of leadership in corporate relocations

- Third, a *People Person* who is able and willing to relate, with empathy, to relocatees and their concerns throughout the relocation period. This calls for people skills: interest in people, helping skills (empathy, facilitation and problem solving), and the authority and confidence to act on their behalf.

Not surprisingly, these roles are not easily compatible. The psychological aptitudes and the required experiences cannot easily be found in one person. This, in turn, has implications for the management of relocation processes. We will come back to it at the concluding part of this chapter.

We will follow the relocation process by arranging our data and commentary around five periods (Figure 4.2):

1. The decision to relocate.
2. The announcement of relocation.
3. The transition period between announcement and the physical relocation.
4. The relocation event itself and the post-relocation period.

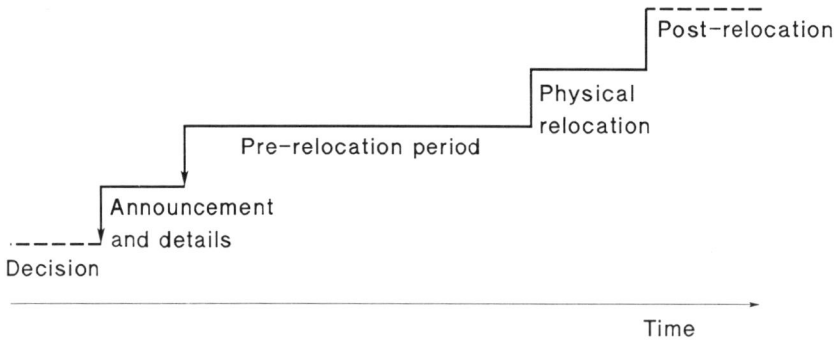

Figure 4.2   Key steps of a relocation schedule

DECIDING TO RELOCATE

Unfortunately, not much is known about the process involved in reaching a decision to relocate. It is much easier to follow developments, once a decision has been taken and processes become overt. Except on those rare occasions when the decision to relocate itself is debated in public, the reasons and arguments for and against remain locked behind closed (boardroom) doors. The data we have access to are *post facto* only and suggest the following:

1. The driving factors are rarely human resources (HR) related. Most commonly it will have to do with rent and rates, space and access routes. HR issues will, if at all, be secondary con-

cerns and taken into account when considering location options. Of particular relevance would be costs: relocation to an area where labour costs are cheaper would be seen as an advantage; and skills availability—particularly where highly developed technical skills are required.

2. Consultations are restricted to board level, with not more than half a dozen top executives involved. One can only wonder whether a "groupthink" phenomenon is not bound to occur. (Groupthink is a phenomenon in which the norm for consensus overrides the realistic appraisal of alternative courses of action.) The Human Resources department seldom occupies a seat on the board and therefore HR issues are not likely to be debated.

3. Deliberations are often held in confidence and commercial firms are likely to view them as "top secret". As a result, the quality of the decision reached is a reflection on the top decision makers in the organization. Little external advice will be allowed to filter through.

MANAGING THE ANNOUNCEMENT

Officially, relocation starts rolling from the moment the formal announcement is made, usually delivered by the Managing Director or the Chief Executive Officer. However, relocation *really* starts the moment the informal grapevine has been informed and the rumours reach a large enough number of employees who are (potentially) affected by it. In all the cases we reviewed, rumours concerning relocation had been circulating for considerable periods of time before the formal announcement was made. In one instance, where only the location was an unknown (because of expiry of lease, relocation was a certainty), the grapevine was fully aware of options considered, by following the project manager's daily movements (through an unsuspecting secretary).

When To Announce?

The time span between announcement and the actual start of physical relocation varies considerably. The longest we found was five years for a government department and the shortest was six weeks for a telecommunication company. Differences are due to economic sectors. Rightly or wrongly, leaders of commercial enterprises try to keep news of this sort close to their chests; there seems also a tendency for faster moving industries to cut down on the time lapse between announcement and relocation. We know of a food retailer who expects its managers (though not whole work units) to relocate within *days* of a decision being taken.

Necessarily, the attitude of top management to the timing of the announcement reflects a deep-seated value orientation to its employees. The difference between *assets* and *resources* comes to mind. If employees are seen to be *assets* then there is no qualitative difference between them and other assets: a building, say. In which case, it seems logical to coincide a decision over a building to informing employees. As a manager in a public company commented: "we were actually building buildings so it was not feasible to keep it quiet". If, on the other hand, the people of an organization are perceived to be *resources*, rather than *assets*, then advising them about forthcoming changes in their lives, in the earliest conceivable time, would seem to be a logical step.

Unjustified Fears and Long-Term Damage

Companies tend to delay announcing the relocation until the very last moment in the belief that, if too much notice is given, then those employees who are not going to relocate would quit immediately, thus leaving the company short-staffed during a critical period. In market conditions of high demand and in occupations of high mobility, this might be the case—although, I hasten to add, we found no evidence to that effect. On the other hand, we found considerable evidence of the damage inflicted by a belated announcement. These are just a few examples:

● The working of rumours. It is safe to assume that the unofficial grapevine often knows of an impending relocation earlier than management expect. However, this knowledge may not be accurate. It is not unusual for rumours to be exaggerated, and the time before a rumour turns into malicious gossip is short. Both are reactions to uncertainties and fears. Without official confirmation, individuals concerned lack crucial information. For example, they do not know whether they are going to be asked to relocate, what kind of remuneration package will be offered, and if there are any structural/organizational changes planned, etc.

- Damage to manager–employee relations. A manager who was informed, officially, six months before a relocation was formally announced, discloses his difficulties in coping with the conflicting pressures put on him: "I was unable to deny or confirm rumours or honestly answer direct questions from my staff. When the general announcement was finally made I felt that I personally lost credibility in the eyes of my staff, who believed that I should have confided in them."

- Damage to industrial relations. "What would you do if you thought that your company did not consider it important to advise about your future and your family's future as early as it possibly could?" a junior manager availed. Although that was by no means a general concern, we were left in no doubt as to most employees preferences for an early announcement and a general attitude of concern for those affected by the decision.

- Damage to wider familial/communal relations. The family is the first to feel the effect of persistent rumours of relocation: the spouse is becoming nervous about his/her work situation; children are getting restless and start contemplating the consequences for their lives; any major family plans are put on hold.

Positive Rewards

Instead of contemplating the penalty for the company if employees leave because they have been given long notice (which allows them to shop around), why not consider a *positive reward* approach instead? One company offered "loyalty payments" for those staff who would not leave until the date of relocation.

How Early Is Not Too Early?

While an early announcement is better than a late one, a premature announcement might be a problem. To explain why this is so, I have to make a brief diversion into the domain of cultural anthropology to borrow an idea called "rites of passage".

Relocation as a rite of passage

Rites of passage are a set of cultural transformation rituals, concerning key change events in the lives of individuals, which also have wider community implications. Birth, puberty, marriage and death are universal change events, conforming to a remarkably similar pattern of rites of passage among widely dispersed cultures.

There are structures common to all rites of passage. First, separation from a given position (status, role); second, certain physical and symbolic steps are taken to transfer the individual concerned into the new position; and third, upon assuming the new position (status, role) participants are ceremoniously returned to normal routine.

The transformation from one stage in life to another is a process that usually involves a transition period. During the transition period, the individual concerned can be very vulnerable. He or she has made a commitment to change from one particular position (status, role) to another, but although the first steps have been taken, the transformation is still incomplete. The person involved has yet to assume their new position (status, role). The transition period is characterized by uncertainty, tension, doubts and fear of failure. It is as though one is on a journey, having left one's point of departure but not yet reached one's destination. There is, therefore, a universal tendency to make the transition period as short as possible, so as to reduce the negative aspects associated with the change and so reduce the probability of something going wrong.

A relocation can be equated with a rite of passage. It involves a change of location usually associated with a fundamental change for the individual concerned and his/her family (moving house, job, school; changing scene/environment; leaving friends and relatives). More often than not, a relocation is also used as an opportunity to create some organizational changes. In short, there are all the reasons to regard it as a life transforming event.

More Than Six Weeks and Less Than Five Years

As in all rites of passage, the transformation period is the most vulnerable of the entire process. It would therefore be of advantage to all concerned if it was to be shorter rather than longer: which brings us back to the question "how early is too early?". On the face of it, wouldn't it be better to make the transformation as swift as possible? Wouldn't it be better to be done and get through with relocation in one quick swoop?

Well, a six weeks' notice period given in one company was considered far too short in the opinion of our interviewees. Employees felt that they were under stress induced by a lack of time to prepare. They reported feeling preoccupied with the problems of coping with what was essentially a crisis situation: how to rearrange life and commitments in six weeks.

At the other extreme, people can have too long to prepare. Employees can experience stress created by an over-extended transition period. A five-year notice period given by one company we surveyed was considered by employees to be too disruptive to organizational routine.

What is the optimum time span between announcement and actual relocation? Well, the answer is that we really can't tell. The decision is too dependent on varying circumstances, as well as on expectations (based on past and comparable experiences of employees) and cultural (organizational and national) conventions. But since you are unlikely to be satisfied with such a reply, for the average company in the UK a time span of 18–24 months between announcement and relocation is about right. For a comparable US company a somewhat shorter time span might be in order.

The "Cry Wolf" Syndrome

One of the risks of too lengthy a transition period is, like in any prolonged rite of passage, that the final destination may never be reached. A combination of unforeseen circumstances and time itself may make the change obsolete. If that happens, any future change programme will be met with scepticism. If, in a history of an organization, too many change programmes do not materialize, then the "cry wolf" syndrome may take over.

In one organization we studied, not atypical of other former public sector institutions, the "cry wolf" syndrome was enshrined in the organization's culture. By this we mean that decisions (of different kind and order) would be made and announced, but before implementation was due, they would be changed, postponed or cancelled altogether.

When the decision to relocate the organization was announced, it was greeted with the by now familiar *déjà vu* nod. The Chief Executive Officer, being aware of the traditions of the past, took the unusual step of specifying the exact date for relocating, some 18 months later. He consciously attempted to strike at the "cry wolf" phenomenon. Unintentionally he nearly trapped himself and his organization since the building which was initially chosen was not ready on schedule. The Chief Executive Officer had to decide whether to postpone the relocation for some time: he decided against it. Instead, he opted for another building elsewhere in order to keep to the original timetable. It was less convenient, it necessitated some unforeseen adjustments and created several disappointments (relocatees purchasing a house in proximity to the first building) but the alternative was apparently perceived to be worse. Relocation was completed by the announced date.

Making the Announcement

The means is the message

The general consensus among companies, relocation agencies and employees, is that it is for the most senior officer in the organization to convey a message of such importance—the Chief Executive Officer or the Managing Director—and to convey it verbally. It not only is in line with the office to be bearer of such news, but it also manifests the support of that office to the move: support which is essential for its success.

In large organizations, it may be impossible or impractical to convey the message *personally*. A good alternative is a video announcement to be screened in tandem at the different work sites and, preferably, a copy handed out to each employee (allowing one to listen to it more than once and an efficient way to pass on the message to the family).

Another option employed is to circulate a memorandum. In one major company, where a photocopied memorandum was used, it proved disastrous to morale. After all, you expect a personal touch when a major decision affecting your life and the life of those dearest to you, is communicated.

The great advantage of a personal, verbal communication, is the opportunity afforded to employees to ask questions. After all, a message, no matter how clear and detailed, may not cover all aspects important to the people concerned. In addition, hearing a message of such personal import once only can often result in its contents not being grasped entirely. The opportunity to ask questions, preferably of as high an office as possible, is fundamental to ensuring that no misunderstandings occur. A question and answer session, following the announcement, is an opportunity to demonstrate the leadership such an occasion calls for ("follow me", "trust me—I know what I'm doing"). It is also an opportunity to air some of the concerns in public, thereby sharing the experience and enhancing the groups' solidarity.

Timing

The precise *timing* of the announcement is of relatively little consequence, in comparison with the time scales involved. However, the exception concerns advising against a particular practice which has been found to be rather common: announcing the relocation on Friday afternoon, immediately prior to employees' leaving for the weekend. The reasons behind this practice are not difficult to guess: at the end of the working week, the interference with work that the announcement will confer is minimal; also, employees will have the whole weekend to digest the news and discuss it with their families.

However, leaving employees for an entire weekend (Friday p.m. to Monday a.m.) without, perhaps, *all* the details, without an opportunity to ask questions, debate and share the experience, resulted in adverse effects: anxiety levels were raised, frustration mounted and rumours, that is, unsustainable information, flourished. Far from being a conducive facilitator, the weekend turns into a stressful event. Please, don't announce a move at 2.00 p.m. on Friday. This is the surest way to start a most complicated change programme on the wrong footing.

THE TRANSITION PERIOD BETWEEN ANNOUNCEMENT AND ACTUAL RELOCATION: KEY CONCERNS AND HOW TO MANAGE THEM

The Day After

The day after the announcement is Day One for the relocation. Nothing is the same again. From now on, each employee lives in two worlds: carrying on with their tasks, while contemplating the future. An organizational change process has begun, and the organization had better be prepared for it.

The following should be prepared and handy: a clearly presented rationale for the move, a clear commitment as to the shape of the new organization, a detailed relocation package, and a framework to deal with enquiries. However, this rarely happens. This is partly because on so many occasions there is a perceived need for secrecy, and partly because Personnel (Human Resources) are rarely in a position to lead decisions of that kind and are unlikely to be advised early enough to be adequately prepared.

A Relocation Administration

Ideally, the relocation programme requires an administration of its own, detached from routine organizational functions and structures. An outline for an effective administration is illustrated in Figure 4.3.

The administration is comprised of three functions:

1. Project management, which is largely an external function: liaison with the agencies responsible for preparing the new site.

2. A public relations, "salesmanship", function aimed at manufacturing and communicating updated information on the state of the relocation.

3. A "people person" function, which attends to the enquiries, concerns and requests of potential relocatees.

More often than not, it is one person (or one office) which handles all the above. While close relationship between the three functions is of course necessary, our data suggest that a functional (and symbolic) separation of the functions is preferable.

A project manager is engaged with the outside world. Therefore, he or she is likely to spend progressively more time outside the company. As a result, it will become increasingly difficult for them to find the time to manage internal affairs. A PR/sales function needs to "sell" the project to internal customers (the company's staff) as well as to external agencies. One can hardly expect this function to do a credible job in relating to employee concerns and providing effective counselling. (A PR job is highly visible; a counselling function aims to keep a low, discreet profile.) Indeed, complaints of "overselling" and unreliable information were associated with a confusion between a PR/sales function and a counselling function.

Last but not least, the three functions are psychologically incompatible. It is not easy to reconcile a people approach (counselling employees) with a task mission (project management) and the intangibilities of selling an image (the PR function). As suggested in Figure 4.3, all three should be directly accountable to the Chief Executive Officer/Board and should operate independently of the existing command structure.

The Importance of Direct Communications

In any change programme, it is essential to control and manage corporate communication. Change requires informing, explaining,

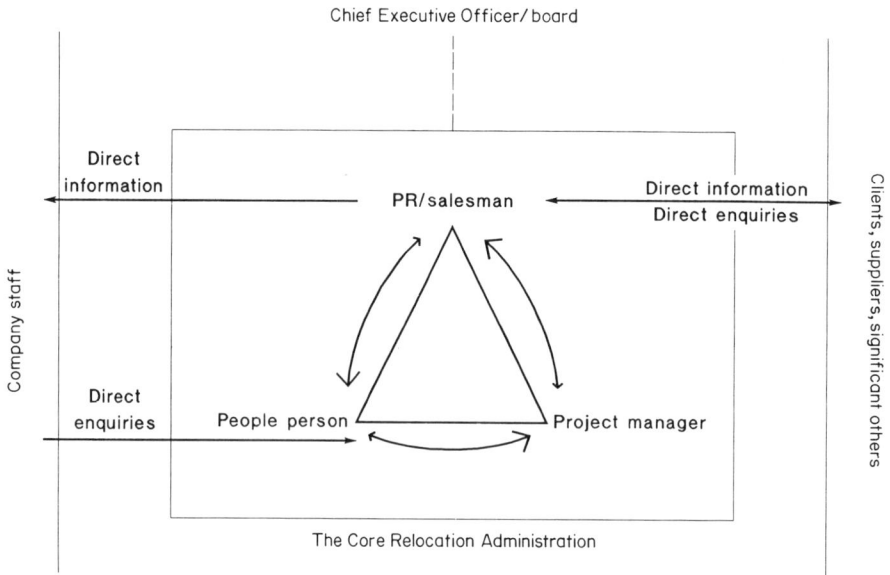

Figure 4.3   An outline of an effective administrative structure for managing relocations

persuading. Four pitfalls stand in the way of effective communication in this instance.

1. The length of the process: relocation is a series of unfolding events over many months.

2. The use of existing communication channels.

3. The efficiency with which communications filter down the chain of command.

4. The "noise" created by those who object (actively or passively) to the change.

The length of the change programme calls for periodical updating. Beyond the obvious informative aspects, there is also a relevant symbolic aspect to capitalize on. The progress of a building (whether it is construction or refurbishing) is a positive manifestation of change (as is any act of creation).

The use of existing communication channels for the relocation exercise is not recommended. Too many internal publications (more than PR people would like to admit) find their way to the bin, unread. A *new* publication may attract more attention and is yet another way to alert staff to the change programme; as well as manifesting the detachment of the relocation administration from existing structures.

For the information to be precise, it should be direct. Information that passes along a chain of command is bound to result in some inaccuracies and confusion. In one company, the important decisions were passed through the chain of command (the less important news were conveyed by memo or newsletter). The results were less than satisfactory. An "open information" policy, together with direct communication to all concerned, would tackle this problem effectively.

Lastly, direct communication will overcome the (direct and indirect) influence of those in the company who "drag their feet". The same mentioned company found that the flow and tone of communications were interfered with by some managers who were less enthusiastic about the move.

THE RELOCATION PACKAGE

The only area in corporate relocations where professional advice can be obtained easily is the designing and executing of financial relocation packages (to include technical aspects, removals, house purchase, school search, even job search for the spouse). Many a consultant makes their living from administering relocation packages and we would not like to add to the plethora, but to point out (with the risk of reiterating the obvious) some observations.

- *Make it simple*: make clear, uncomplicated regulations and put them in simple, user-friendly terms. You will be surprised how many people have a far from satisfactory command of the language. Legal language may create an involuntary reluctance to deal with "the small print".

- *Make it universal*: as much as possible, apply the same rules to everyone, thereby creating a shared experience, which will consolidate the people who move. Even in multi-tier bureaucracies, a common relocation package would be acceptable, while a differential package may create resentment and divisions.

- *Make it flexible*: different people have different needs. As long as the basics are universal, the constituent parts of a package could differ to suit individual requirements. For example, a counselling function with the power to authorize arrangements would prove invaluable.

- *Have it ready in time*: every so often, the formal structure of the company relocation package is not available at the time the announcement is made. Worse, in some companies we have come across, details are changed and commitments altered. This is wrong. It fails to reinforce a positive attitude towards the move, it puts in question the ability and leadership of management, and it throws the future of employees into confusion.

At the beginning of this chapter we characterized relocation as an organizational crisis, from which most of those involved emerge relatively unharmed. This says something about the resilience of the average human being. It also suggests that, as a company, *provided you get the most important things right, it does not matter what else you do—you can even get a few things wrong*. A relocation package is one of those things which you had better get right. It is the minimum employees expect of you.

PREPARING FOR THE MOVE

While the relocation itself, the actual move, can be rightly described as a traumatic event, it can nevertheless be cushioned by taking adequate preparatory steps. There are two main areas: in the work context and in the wider community context.

Preparing for the New Work Reality

Building news update

This was a common feature in the companies we studied. Photos, trivia and commentary are useful in conveying a picture of the emerging new reality. It also helps in keeping the move in focus.

Better still, if those interested can visit the building site, to form their own impressions: tangibility is the best way to ensure preparedness.

A model office

One of the companies we studied created a real size model of an office in the new building, and invited all to see and comment, partly for informative purposes, partly as a consultative exercise. This proved very popular.

Participation in internal design

Here is an opportunity to involve staff in creating the new work environment, by active engagement in the making of the internal design. A popular item for consultation is the *office chair*. Which chair to opt for in the new building is a matter of some interest to those who will occupy it. As many companies take advantage of relocation to instil a *corporate image* (even if they did not see a need for it before), they aim for a unitary type of chair and staff are invited to cast their vote.

This is a positive exercise, but it carries three health warnings:

1. It absorbs a great deal of time and energy: be prepared (and accordingly, assign the *people person* rather than the *project manager* to deal with it).

2. Take it seriously: make sure you allow everyone to try out the available options and cast their vote, publicize the results, and—most importantly—follow the majority ruling (and do not allow the chairman's wife to overturn the decision).

3. Don't overdo it, since after all it's only a marginal aspect of the whole operation, and staff may call the bluff, namely: the real decisions are taken elsewhere, while they have to be content with the choice of a chair.

A final note: indeed, why not engage staff in the internal design of the building? Why not involve them in deciding the colour scheme, decoration, patterns for the dining room and the shapes of the telephones? There is no better way of bringing people closer to the change event itself and preparing them for things to come.

Getting to know new colleagues

A new building is often used as a means of rationalizing operations by bringing together geographically remote units. These do not necessarily possess a similar professional or even organizational culture (though belonging to the same company). The shock of moving into a new work environment will be exacerbated by having to accommodate unfamiliar style and work habits (this is particularly true for a smaller or less powerful unit joining up with a bigger or more powerful one). As such an amalgamation is likely to be planned well in advance, what could be easier than providing the opportunity for bringing people together by organizing, for example, a joint visit to the new location?

Preparing for the new community

While most companies do some work related preparations prior to the move, few cast a wider view which includes the community as well. The result is that far too often relocatees feel as if they have been deserted in the wilderness. Two complaints are common. First, too little time off work is granted to familiarize with the new locality. While one or two organized trips (over the weekend) for relocating personnel are the norm, a tourist's gaze is not the best way to learn what it is like living in a place. When the existing location is distant from the new one, getting the time to explore the new community becomes a major problem. The companies we studied were not able to deal with that satisfactorily. The result: far too often the relocating family is shell-shocked into the new community.

The second major problem is being dependent on interested parties for vital information. These interested parties include estate agents, the relocation agency and the local development corporation. Their advice is perceived as biased and partial. If on top of that the company's approach is one of "oversell" (the PR function dominates), the company's information credibility also becomes undermined. Under such circumstances, staff are at loss.

The solution is a simple one, yet our data suggest it is rarely used: *networking*, i.e. making connections between employees and local residents. Any community has numerous voluntary organizations/interests groups/clubs, whose members will only be happy to provide assistance to newcomers by plugging them into the network of impartial know-how: tips for choosing a neighbourhood, the "right" school and even the "real" house prices. It has not been unknown for a cartel of local estate agents to gang up on relocating employees, raising house prices by up to 20% (in the good old days of the late 1980s, that was). These two evils, lack of time and lack of knowledge, far too often combine together to effect a costly mistake: choosing the wrong location/house/school.

A more elaborate form of information networking is *befriending* or *buddying*. This is for relocatees who are particularly vulnerable: they need not only friendly advice but also a friendly hand. A not untypical case is that of a junior supervisor in his early twenties, working for a major blue chip company, who was relocating from an inner London borough, where he lived at home with his parents, to his first ever flat in a housing estate in the wastelands of Milton Keynes. The poor man was at a total loss. A local "buddy", whether in the community, or, better, the company, would have made all the difference. But to make it happen you need, first, the right function to identify the problem (a *people person*) and second, the appropriate company policy to facilitate it.

MANAGING THE SYMBOLIC

A Note on Symbolism in Organizational Life during Times of Change

We resorted to symbolism before, when discussing the time dimension of the transition period, equating it to a "rite of passage". There is a further note to make in this regard, concerning organizations in general.

An organization is made up of various facets. There is the physical-structural component (buildings), the people component (staff, customers, suppliers, contractors), the task component (mission, plans, operations, achievements), the process component (any inter-active throughputs: from production to interpersonal) and the symbolic component.

Unlike all other components, which are tangible to different degrees, the symbolic component of an organization is not. It is not tangible because it exists only in the minds of people. It cannot be con-strued objectively, it cannot be validated, because it changes as times and circumstances and people change. Nevertheless it forms an important part of the organizational reality. Furthermore, in times of change, the symbolic component assumes a major role because, as stated earlier, a transition period is associated with ambiguity and uncertainty, creating tension, doubts and fear of failure. It is in these circumstances that people attach themselves to intangibles and where an extra dimension is added to routine processes and daily objects.

A chair, a desk, a room are more than just functional objects. We will notice these added aspects as newcomers into an organization and quickly forget them as we stride into routine. But in changing circumstances, the added meanings to these and other objects, pro-cedures and routines, surface again and become an important part of our reality. This is why choosing a new chair becomes more than just an exercise in participative design; why a vaguely written relo-cation package turns into a confidence test for management; why the size of an assigned office is taken as an omen for things to come and one's space slot in the future underground car park relative to the position of the lift of the newly built office complex becomes a structural map of organizational politics.

Not that these symbolic aspects were absent before, but the impor-tance attached to them and the meaning conferred upon them has become magnified. A relocation unfreezes the status quo in the organization. It is an intangible change. On the surface, nothing is different: routines, people, objects are the same. In reality they are not. The new situation transforms the organization, through the allusions of people, into a different one. The rearrangement of positions and people, the new possibilities and alternatives, mean that business is not as usual. Understanding that is a prerequisite to managing this period of transition successfully.

Managing the Symbolic in the Transition Period

Making change visible

Between announcing the relocation to actually moving takes a long time, sometimes up to 5 years (although the average is about 18 months). During that time, one of the challenges to management is how to keep relocation high on the organizational agenda. Seemingly, this is a paradox. Surely, such a critical event is not going to escape the attention of those concerned. Perhaps not, but then there is the daily routine to keep you busy and sometimes it is easier to repress the inevitable than to confront it, by delaying dealing with a new reality. Finally, some organizations have a tradition of change that never materializes (the "cry wolf" phenomenon).

To combat this, the forthcoming change has to be made visible. One way of doing this is by creating a special task force to administer the relocation programme, discussed earlier in a different context. An important feature of the separate administration is that it has its own channels of communication, distinct from the normal organizational channels. Common practice is to use some form of newsletter, but increasingly use is being made of edited videos which bring home the images of change (construction progress, information on the new locality).

Another way of increasing the unit's visibility is by creating a special *language of change*: new words, acronyms, nicknames, that become routinized in the organization's operations, and have a specific bearing to the forthcoming relocation.

Managing anxiety

At the end of the day, the transition period is a prolonged waiting for the unknown. Various means can be, and should be, employed to bring the future closer to home by preparing for it (as elaborated before) but until you cross the bridge you don't know what awaits you at the other end.

A major cause for concern is the impact the relocation will have on *my* job. First, the relocation *may* go disastrously wrong with who knows what consequences; second, companies have a tendency to see the relocation as a prime opportunity for reorganization (which of course it is). Reorganization these days means, more often than not, shedding jobs. What if it happens to *me*?

We speculate about the future from information concerning the present. The company's future commitment to us, and its treatment of those staff who do not relocate are important indicators. One imaginative way of dealing with anxieties of relocation is by making a visible effort to help staff who stay behind. A company that did just that, investing heavily in counselling the staff who did not relocate, offering them alternative employment and handing them a generous redundancy package, was in fact sending a message to its relocating employees: trust us. See how we care for staff about to leave. Imagine how important we consider you. Our study confirmed that people got the message.

THE PHYSICAL RELOCATION

How Many D-Days?

The D-Day has arrived. The organization relocates. In one day, two or more? The technical, operational and financial concerns dictate the answer and rightly so. But it is worth noting that a phased relocation (if technically, operationally and financially viable) may have some merits.

First, it is safe to assume that something–somewhere–somehow is going to go wrong. Having a margin of time to correct things would take pressure off the process. Second, the first wave of relocatees is hit hardest. Following waves benefit from the lessons of the first. Therefore, there is something to be said for making the first wave smaller, composed of relocation enthusiasts (all other things being equal) who will send back positive feedback.

Third, enabling relocatees to choose their own timing has some indirect benefits (that is, symbolical rather than practical). It makes their move more of volition than by dictate, it allows some freedom of choice and therefore makes the move a conscientious effort. That is good for organizational commitment.

The Enigma of Open Space Offices

More and more companies relocate to open space offices, lured by reduced costs and a greater flexibility. Most realize that an open space office is not simply a different spatial arrangement, but implies a certain management style and corporate culture—namely, of open communications and participative management. It is unfortunate, however, that a relocation is usually managed in a manner that is contrary to what a participative culture requires.

First, *consultations*. We have not come across a single case where consultations with staff on matters concerning the relocation were actively encouraged. In fact, most decisions, starting with the cardinal decision of location and ending with the internal colour scheme, are decided in a small forum of key decision makers.

Second, *corporate image*. The move to a new building is seized upon to renew the corporate image. In an open plan scheme, this is achieved by standardizing furniture, colour schemes, dress code and routine regulations. Unless all that is done by participative decision making (which it usually is not) it will only undermine the credibility of management.

Relocation and Reorganization

A relocation is a major organizational change in its own right, but also an opportunity to drive structural and operational changes. Should it be seized upon? There are arguments for and against.

On the positive side, a strategic re-examination, if required, is surely a good thing and relocation would be a good time to execute it. Also, being in a process of change facilitates the introduction of all sorts of changes as the justification is often self-explanatory.

On the negative side, adjustment to, and coping with, more than one change is difficult and disruptive. If multiple changes occur consecutively it will prolong the recovery to normality, as people start a second change cycle before completing the first.

While most change programmes these days aim to encourage *initiative*, relocation is managed in a manner that encourages *dependency*.

All major decisions are imposed upon employees, starting with the very decision of the company to relocate, the location, timing, compensation package. One is left with little opportunity for initiative. Hence, driving a change programme during relocation may not be well received.

Displaced Frustration

A common feature of the physical relocation is the "who gets the new furniture and who does not" scenario. There will always be some people who get new furniture, and some who do not but think they should have done. There are perfectly good reasons for giving to Jack but not to Jim, yet it still causes a great deal of resentment.

Having come across the same scenario in several companies drives me to attribute it to the dependency instigated by the move, i.e. if management gives to Jack, why shouldn't it give to Jim? Since Jim cannot get angry for being dictated to on the *big* decisions, at least he can get angry on marginal injustices: *in times of change the symbolic reigns.*

POST-RELOCATION BLUES

By many accounts, the period immediately after relocation is the most difficult one. The work-place is not yet settled, the family is just starting to find its place in the new locality and there is always something that is not quite right.

However, the worst is over. The relocation has taken place, the physical move is completed and the settling in period takes its normal course. From a management point of view the task is finished. Or is it? The research reviewed in earlier chapters of this book suggests that adjustment to a move can take anything up to 18 months.

Where specialist functions have been established to deal with ongoing problems during a group move, the best advice would appear to be "keep things going". As with adjustment to many significant life events, what follows immediately after is, to some extent, a temporary reaction. The novelty of living in new surroundings, the excitement of a new home and a new job can often mask underlying anxieties. It is not until this "honeymoon" period is over that the realities of change begin to sink in. Not being able to find one's way about, not having friends to go out with, feeling that the company has forced this move on employees without telling them about how this would feel; these can all contribute to feelings of anxiety and homesickness.

It is just as important that these feelings be dealt with quickly at this stage as they were during the early days of a move. Organizations can help in ways already discussed. Setting up social groups, encouraging wider participation among family members and even, in more extreme cases, providing individual counselling. Post-relocation blues are a reality for many people. Apart from the obvious impact they can have on individual employee performance, where organizations are phasing a move over several months, stories of the problems faced by the first waves of relocatees can soon filter back to those yet to move. Evidently the provision of some sort of ongoing support over the first year or two can prove cost effective for many organizations who have undertaken a successful corporate relocation.

CHAPTER 5　International aspects of job relocation in the 1990s

INTRODUCTION

Growing numbers of British companies are intent on increasing their presence in both continental European and global markets in the 1990s. Sixty-two per cent of a group of 171 organizations surveyed in 1990 planned to expand their business interests into Europe. For the men and women working in these organizations, international careers are becoming increasingly common.

From a practical point of view, applied research into the impact of overseas postings on employees and their families is only in its infancy. Only a handful of studies in this area were published during the 1970s and 1980s. However, the indications are that this situation is rapidly changing. Mainstream professional journals, such as the *Academy of Management Review*, are turning their attention to relevant issues concerning the international dimensions of human resource management (HRM) and the experiences of expatriate managers returning to their countries of origin. A number of books aimed at management and business audiences also address these important and topical issues.

Recent economic and social events in Europe have put international relocation much higher on the business agenda. The advent of the Single European Market, along with rapid social and economic change in eastern bloc countries, will inevitably accelerate present levels of job mobility within and between national borders. It is certain that international career pathing and mobility will become a much more common feature of the working lives of British managers and professionals, male and female.

This chapter sets out to examine international job mobility under three headings: first, we will look at why multinational organizations use expatriate relocation as part of their business strategy, how current practice is likely to be influenced by the advent of the Single European Market, and the financial cost of all this movement to the employer. Secondly, we will consider the psychological impact of international moves on employees and their families, why some people find the process difficult, and the problems of predicting in advance whether a move will end in success or failure. Finally, a review of research concerning good international relocation management will examine the issues of selection, training and ongoing support from the perspective of the human resource department.

CORPORATE RELOCATION POLICY AMONG THE MULTINATIONALS

Why move people between countries?

International mobility is common among multinational organizations. Furthermore, the demand for managers and professionals willing to move between countries and cultures is growing. Given the time and trouble it takes to move a valued employee from one country to another, why do companies bother? What are the advantages of having an expatriate move in to do a job rather than recruiting locals? In many cases the advantages are few. For example, sales and marketing functions are often best left to members of the host nation. They will have an unrivalled grasp of the specialist knowledge concerning customs and protocols necessary to oil the wheels of business exchange. For example, an expatriate sales executive could easily lose a valuable contract with an Arab client should he or she turn down an invitation to their home. Information concerning cultural differences of this sort is often left out of formal training and preparation for international assignments.

Evidently there needs to be sound economic reasoning behind company policy on expatriation. The most obvious reason for posting an employee overseas is the need for their specialist skills. This situation is most common within those companies dealing with state of the art technology. For example, electronics, engineering and computer industries often have teams of trouble-shooters who can be called in either to establish or to maintain specialist systems that local professionals are unfamiliar with. While longer term solutions can involve training host nationals to perform these functions, there is often a temporary skills gap that has to be filled via international relocation.

Just as domestic relocation is used as a tool to provide managerial talent with a wide range of experience within an organization, so international mobility is used to develop similar managerial skills. Multinational organizations need executives with appropriate experience of their world markets. To fulfil this need, the careers of these high-flyers are planned to include foreign postings. By the time a manager comes to hold an executive position at head office, he or she will have acquired not just valuable experience in overseas subsidiaries, but also personal contacts with local management.

In addition to delivering specialist skills and providing managers with experience, international relocation is used by the multinationals to establish and maintain corporate control over newly created or acquired subsidiaries. Establishing a style of management consistent with the culture and climate within head office is a very important first step in any new operation. This evidently requires the attention of someone well versed in the workings of the parent company. Their function is usually to create and develop new management teams, to ensure that these teams are aware and capable of executing corporate strategy formulated at head office, and to build an effective, efficient and loyal work-force.

This brief review of how international mobility fits into the corporate plans of multinationals gives the first clue to some of the difficulties faced by expatriates. While they are, first and foremost, representatives of the parent company, expatriate managers often face the daunting task of having to win the hearts and minds of local employees in order to achieve their goals. Where corporate policy and local interests come into conflict, it is often the expatriate who is caught between the two. Thus the importance of careful planning and adequate preparation when it comes to successful international relocation becomes evident.

1992 and All That

The end of 1992 sees the beginning of the Single European Market. Nothing since the invention of the telephone has preoccupied the business pages of newspapers and magazines in such an all embracing manner.

The debate rages around the extent to which the economic changes due to sweep across Europe will influence corporate practice in Britain. A popular vision is one of an ill-prepared business community being overwhelmed by competitors from France, Germany and the like. Survey results confirm the hypothesis. Forty per cent of British organizations claim to have some specific corporate plan aimed at the Single European Market, compared with 80% of their European competitors. Of the British entrepreneurs questioned, most appeared to be concerned about protecting home markets rather than developing new ones. The conclusion reached by subscribers to this school of thought is that the negative attitude towards the Single European Market so typical of the British is a monumental, and potentially fatal, error of judgement.

Alternatively, other observers point to the fact that British companies have been trading in Europe for centuries, and that the Single European Market is set to change very little in existing business practice.

Whoever might be right in their predictions, the fact of the matter is that corporate business activity by British companies in Europe is taking an upturn. In response to economic changes, many companies are instituting policies that include wide reaching reorganization and rationalization. New operations are being established on the European mainland, or existing ones being acquired through mergers and acquisitions.

Not all of this activity is due directly to the establishing of a single market. Many of the larger multinational corporations are responding to what they believe to be a new pan-European business climate by establishing new regional centres that will benefit from the inevitable growth and improvement in communication and transport infrastructures across the continent.

The numbers of people involved in international mobility expands or contracts in response to corporate demands for geographical expansion. The Single European Market represents perhaps the biggest demand for economic expansion since the Marshall Plan. Add to this the radical economic and social changes that are taking place in Eastern Europe, and the scene is set for a dramatic rise in the demand for highly mobile employees capable of moving, adapting and working successfully in foreign countries.

The Financial Costs

One of the few facts concerning international relocation that can be stated without fear of contradiction is that *it is expensive*. Just how much it costs to relocate an expatriate manager and his or her family is extremely difficult to estimate. Obviously it depends on many different factors: over what distance is the move? how long is the employee staying? what kind of remunerations and benefits are offered by the employer? etc. In an article published in 1990, Jean-Marie Hiltrop and Maddy Janssens estimated that the average cost of an international relocation was between US$ 55 000 and US$ 150 000.

With each move costing so much, the price of a failed international assignment is high. Not only are the costs of the initial move lost, there are the additional costs of early repatriation, to say nothing of the damage that may have been done to the relationship between the employing organization and a valued employee. Managers of the calibre likely to be offered international relocations often represent a great deal of investment on behalf of their companies. Several years of training and grooming for senior management costs money. Should the employee feel that their move was badly managed, that investment might be lost to a competitor.

Given the importance of international mobility to corporate planning, and the expense involved, the rates at which these moves go wrong are surprisingly high. As many as four out of every ten managers moved to a foreign location fail to reach the end of their assignment. It has further been estimated that between 50% and

80% of American managers perform less effectively than usual while working abroad. The reasons given are either poor work performance and/or an inability to adjust to the host nation. Problems with the management of international relocation costs organizations based in the USA in excess of two billion dollars every year. Comparable figures for companies based in the UK are unavailable only because the relevant research remains to be done. However, if the domestic relocation scene is anything to go by, it is unlikely that the British manage their international relocations any more effectively.

The importance of getting international mobility right is there for all organizations to see. Getting it wrong can be extremely expensive, not only in terms of direct costs, but also in terms of losing valued employees, disrupting overseas corporate development and gaining an unfavourable reputation among those people whom the organization may seek to recruit.

In order to avoid costly mistakes, it is crucial that companies responsible for initiating international moves are aware of the potential trials and tribulations faced by the expatriate manager and his or her family. The next section of this chapter looks at the psychological aspects of moving between countries.

THE PSYCHOLOGICAL CONSEQUENCES OF INTERNATIONAL MOBILITY

Why Do Some People Find Moving Abroad Difficult?

Earlier chapters of this book looked at the problems facing employees and families relocating within national boundaries. Much of the information that has been gathered about the problems of domestic relocation is also applicable to international mobility. This is just as well given that there is very little research specific to international mobility.

To begin with the incidence of problem moves, figures from the USA suggest that around 40% of foreign assignments terminate ahead of schedule. Add to this the figures for those working less effectively than usual, between 50% and 80% of those remaining, and some estimation as to the extent of stress following an international move can be arrived at. On the basis of available information, it is not unreasonable to assume that as many as six out of every ten international moves involve sufficiently high levels of stress so as to precipitate either an early return or at least a significant drop in normal levels of effective functioning at work.

Establishing rates of incidence is one thing, finding causes for the problems facing expatriates is another. Scientists, and social scientists are no exception, are often involved in what are sometimes quite crude summaries and generalizations. When a physicist says that water boils at 100 °C, he or she is making a generalization. Water only boils at that temperature at sea level. However, the generalization is a convenient one that works in most circumstances. Generalizing about such a complex event as an international move is altogether more difficult. It is probably true to say that each move is different, not least because it involves different people moving to different locations for different reasons.

The first step in making some generalizations about the stresses of international mobility is to say something about the various characteristics of a move that create problems. To begin with, what kind of distances are involved? Someone moving from France to The Netherlands, for example, is less likely to experience change comparable with a colleague moving from France to China. Of course it is not just physical distance, but *cultural* distance that is important. A British manager might find adjusting to a move to Australia less difficult than adjusting to a move to Germany, despite the greater physical distances involved. The greater the differences between the two cultures involved, the more difficult the transition is likely to be. This issue of *culture shock* will be dealt with in more detail in the next section.

Length of assignment is likely to be another important factor in successful adjustment. Many expatriates on very short postings of a few months or less decide it is not worth trying to establish new friendships. Before they have a chance to consolidate new relationships it is time to move again. The importance of friendships, or social support, was emphasized in the section on domestic relocation. The effect of these short postings is to encourage feelings of isolation and place people in a situation where they feel they have no one with whom they can talk about potential difficulties. These problems are made worse when, as is common with many short assignments, an employees' family is not moved with them but remains in their country of origin.

Because the motivating factor behind an international relocation is rooted firmly in the arena of work, aspects of the job play a very important role in the process of adjustment. Where a foreign assignment represents a planned step in the career development of a manager, the rewards, be they financial rewards or status rewards, often help to smooth the transition from one country to another. The very fact that these moves are planned provides adequate preparation time for those involved. Similarly, these planned career moves are often for fixed terms, so the employee and his or her family know exactly how long an overseas posting is going to last. Because the situation is predictable, those involved feel more in control of events and therefore less likely to feel helpless and experience stress.

However, not all international moves fall under the umbrella of career development. In many cases a foreign assignment can be the result of an urgent need for specialist skills in a particular region. The potential for disruption and therefore stress is much greater under these circumstances. Very little planning time is available; the employee has less opportunity to make a considered decision about accepting the post. Indeed in many cases the employee may feel that they do not have the option of refusing the move. On arrival, the urgency of the situation may require the employee to work long hours or to travel within the host country's borders. Separation from the rest of the family at this early stage can make adjustment extremely difficult for all involved.

These few examples provide some idea about the complexity of international job moves. Trying to predict or make lists of the potential problems faced by those involved is an almost impossible task. There are probably as many potential problems surrounding international moves as there are international moves.

To generalize, we can say that some people find these moves difficult simply because they involve change. Moving to another country means giving up all that is familiar. Familiarity is very comforting to most people. It means that our environments are predictable and thus safe. There are no unpleasant surprises awaiting us in the corner shop or at the market. Change can bring with it feelings of insecurity, helplessness and therefore stress. The best kind of help that can be given to people under these circumstances is anything that helps render their surroundings more understandable and therefore predictable. That is why preparation for foreign assignments is so important. More will be said about the role of Human Resource professionals in selection and training prior to an international move later in the chapter.

Culture Shock

Culture shock is another of those concepts, like stress, that is frequently used yet little understood. The phrase has its origins in anthropology. It was used to describe the reactions of people making the transition from one culture to another. In as much as culture shock describes a variety of psychological reactions and behaviours, it is probably fair to say that "culture shock is what culture shock does".

Understanding what culture shock does brings us back to the ideas about the comforting nature of familiarity. Moving into an alien culture instantly makes our surroundings less familiar. Simple tasks like catching a bus or posting a letter may involve having to learn new rules of social behaviour. In situations where the rules of engagement are unknown, embarrassing mistakes can be made. Fear of making oneself conspicuous, making a fool of oneself, produces anxiety. This kind of social anxiety carries with it a number of recognizable symptoms. Feelings of inadequacy, lack of confidence, becoming withdrawn, feeling helpless, becoming short tempered; all are signs that can be associated with culture shock.

Fear of making mistakes during the course of everyday life can produce anxiety. The anxiety produced by the possibility of making serious social gaffes at work can be even greater. Saying the wrong thing, refusing an honoured invitation, or even speaking to the wrong people can jeopardize an important business deal. Making

mistakes during a foreign assignment can have longer term implications for a manager's career. Poor performance, subsequent lack
of confidence, and failing job satisfaction can turn a prestigious
foreign assignment into a nightmare.

Most researchers in the area tend to agree that experiencing some
degree of culture shock is a normal and inevitable part of moving
to another country. It is probably best described as part of the anxiety
that frequently goes hand in hand with change of any sort. There is
some debate, however, as to whether culture shock is always a bad
thing. It is true to say that many of those who regularly move
between countries and cultures do so out of choice. The strange-
ness of the new and unfamiliar, rather than being a source of anxiety is, for some people, a stimulating and refreshing change that
presents fresh challenges and opportunities for personal growth
and development. The initial anxiety that comes with living in a
novel environment is part of the excitement and adventure that is
part and parcel of international mobility. It may in fact serve a useful purpose in motivating people to explore unfamiliar surroundings. As soon as the exploration process is underway, people, places,
and rules of interaction become more familiar. As a place and its
people become more familiar, so life becomes more predictable and
thus more comfortable.

However, for some people culture shock is far from positive. It
may be that the initial shock of the new is so great as to be debili-
tating. Rather than being motivated to explore, people simply
withdraw altogether. This can often happen where preparation has
been inadequate. Making the first tentative steps into unfamiliar
surroundings assumes at least some basic level of understanding
and ability to communicate.

Where people have been given no information about local culture
and customs, or have had no help with learning a new language,
exploration is made much more difficult. For these people, the
"expat" community can serve an invaluable function. Mixing with
people from one's own culture can be a comfort in itself. Those
members of the group who have already spent time in the host
nation can also be a very useful source of information and support
during these early stages. However, the danger is that new arrivals
will come to rely exclusively on members of their own expatriate

community for social support. This can often lead to feelings of isolation from host nationals, and a desire to remain separate and avoid integrating with the local community. In the longer term this can lead to resentment and misunderstanding between host and expatriate communities that helps neither group.

There appears to be agreement among the experts that culture shock is a minor form of anxiety that accompanies any kind of change. For some people it can act as a positive stimulus for exploration. For others, culture shock can be just another name for the unbearable stresses and strains that a foreign posting can place on both individuals and their families. The question that remains is how to identify situations in which people are more or less likely to experience problems of adjustment that we may choose to call culture shock.

In their book, *Culture Shock: Psychological Reactions to Unfamiliar Environments*, Furnham and Bochner (1986) come out in favour of four specific theories or explanations of culture shock that might help people prepare for and deal with the psychological aspects of international moves:

1. The potential for culture shock can be expected to be greater where differences between cultures are most extreme. The more change people are expected to deal with, the more likely it is that they will experience problems.

2. Having access to social support is very important. A network of friends and colleagues capable of acting as guides and mentors during the early stages of a foreign assignment helps to ease adjustment. They provide a source of familiar interactions, boost confidence in ability to adjust over time, and can be an invaluable reservoir of local information.

3. The kinds of cultural differences most likely to precipitate problems of adjustment are to do with values or social mores. For example, Japanese culture is based around many different values that are quite alien to westerners. Respect for those that are older than oneself, the concept of saving face, and a different religious philosophy are all part of a rich cultural tradition that can make adaptation to the Japanese way of life a complex process for many business people.

4. Those people most likely to adapt successfully to an international relocation are those who are best able to learn new social skills. Developing the ability to communicate and make friends with host nationals is reckoned to be a good indicator of coping with culture shock.

This final point illustrates very well the confusion surrounding ideas about culture shock. The argument is somewhat circular: culture shock describes the anxiety associated with moving between countries. The best predictor of successful adaptation to culture shock is developing new friends and colleagues among host nationals. However, getting out and about to meet new people is one of the signs that people are adjusting successfully. Culture shock is what culture shock does.

Despite problems of definition, and confusion over causes, a basic understanding of culture shock can help to prepare both employees and their organizations for the potential pitfalls experienced by many expatriates. The lessons to be learned are clear for all concerned. Culture shock is less likely to be a problem for those who are well prepared before arrival, and have access to social support of some kind during the early stages of a new posting. Successful adaptation is closely linked with successful assimilation rather than continued isolation.

Processes of Adjustment

In an effort to understand what happens as people try to adjust to living in a foreign culture, psychologists have attempted to break the process down into stages. One of the more detailed of these "stage theories" comes from Adler, one of the so-called humanistic psychologists.

Adler proposes that adjustment to living in an alien culture can be broken down into five specific stages. The five are:

1. Contact
2. Disintegration
3. Re-integration

4. Autonomy

5. Independence

Adler describes how a new arrival sees the host country and its inhabitants at each of the five different stages. The theory charts changing emotions and behaviours, and offers an interpretation of what is happening to the person.

Stage one is *contact*. At the point of arrival the new country is perceived as different, fascinating. The expatriate is often very excited, gripped by the potential for discovery. Behaviour is consistent with someone whose curiosity and interest have been aroused. Adler suggests that at this very early stage, new arrivals are still very much bound up in their own culture. Happy in the knowledge of who they are and where they belong, differences in a new culture can be looked at from the outside as it were, from the position of a detached non-participant.

At stage two, *disintegration*, the new arrival is no longer a dispassionate observer. They have to actively participate in the daily routine of the host nation. Cultural differences begin to have a direct impact on day-to-day living. Because the rules that govern social and economic interactions are unfamiliar, people often begin to develop the symptoms of mild anxiety discussed in the previous section. Feelings of helplessness, lack of confidence and confusion are common. From behaving like an excited explorer, expatriates can become depressed and withdrawn. This stage is probably closest to what many people term culture shock. Being forced to recognize and deal with cultural changes reinforces the idea that one is suddenly in a minority. Being the odd one out can be extremely uncomfortable. Simultaneously one loses the comfort of familiar ways of living and is thrust into a new and uncertain world often without any tangible sources of support. The only comfort might be that many people view this temporary or transitional phase as part of the normal process of adjustment.

By stage three, *re-integration*, the helplessness and withdrawal of the previous stage is turning to anger. Cultural differences are evaluated in a negative light. The host country is continually being compared to the expatriate's country of origin in an unfavourable light.

People may become hostile, aggressive and fiercely nationalistic. Members of the host nation are viewed with suspicion and mistrust. Although the tendency to reject the host culture and fiercely defend one's own may be uncharacteristic and even unpleasant, Adler claims that it is in fact a vital step towards reasserting one's own feelings of self-worth. Once this process is complete and self-esteem has been restored, expatriates have the self-confidence to start re-evaluating the host culture and looking at it in a more positive light.

Stage four, *autonomy*, sees a return to more characteristic behaviour. People become more relaxed about living in the host country. They have developed the skills and the confidence to deal with locals. They are able to observe cultural differences and appreciate them for what they are, the reflection of another historical, environmental and social legacy. The fear of failure or ridicule in the course of normal social interaction is no longer there. With the passing of that threat comes a more assured and congenial approach to life.

Finally, stage five, *independence*, represents a consolidation of the gains made at the previous stage. Adjustment is complete. Any cultural differences are both accepted and enjoyed. The experience of living in a foreign country is viewed as an opportunity for growth and self-development.

Once again, it is important to reiterate that Adler's stage theory, along with the several other stage theories concerning adaptation to cultural change, is only a generalization. It is not a magic formula for predicting the behaviour of all expatriates. It does, however, go some way towards helping organizations to understand potential problems facing their employees, and employees to understand both their own and their families' behaviour during this difficult time.

To conclude this section on processes of adjustment, successful adaptation appears to hinge around developing the skills necessary to participate fully in the host culture. Many of these skills revolve around the ability to make new friends among host nationals. Learning the local language, mastering local customs, and feeling relaxed and confident among local people are all important tasks. What is more, they all take time. A study of 200 Norwegian students attending American universities suggested that the whole process of adjustment to living in a foreign country takes around

18 to 20 months. While more seasoned travellers may adjust more quickly, our research on domestic relocation suggests that for some people it may take even longer.

Predicting Success and Failure

International relocation is an expensive business for employer organizations. Evidently it is in their best interests to select those people who are most likely to succeed on a foreign assignment. This fact has not been lost on researchers. The quest has been to discover which individual characteristics of both employees and their families can be used in order to predict successful adaptation to living and working abroad. What follows is a brief review of this research and some consideration of the lessons it may hold for those responsible for recruitment and selection of personnel for foreign assignments.

Individual characteristics

It should come as no surprise that characteristics common among successful expatriate managers include outstanding intelligence, a high degree of self-confidence, a strong desire for responsibility and an ability to see jobs through to their conclusion. It should come as no surprise because this description hopefully applies to the vast majority of those men and women responsible for managing large multinational corporations. What the definition fails to explain is why over half of these people achieve less than was expected of them while on foreign assignments.

Other research into the personal characteristics of successful expatriates has little to add. Consider this description from Phatak (1974):

> Ideally, it seems, he (or she) should have the stamina of an Olympic swimmer, the mental agility of an Einstein, the conversational skill of a professor of languages, the detachment of a judge, the tact of a diplomat, and the perseverance of an Egyptian pyramid builder. And if he is going to measure up to the demands of living and working in a foreign country he should also have a feeling for culture; his moral judgements should not be too rigid; he should be able to merge with the local environment with chameleon-like ease; and he should show no sign of prejudice.

No doubt adopting these criteria would make the selection of personnel for international assignments much easier. One would not expect to find more than two or three people answering this description in most large corporations.

One of the largest research studies in this field involved over 1000 Swedish expatriates, living in 26 different host countries. Satisfaction with, and adjustment to, their posting was measured. In addition, information concerning 30 different individual characteristics and circumstances was collected. The results showed that even when all 30 variables were considered, predicting satisfaction and adjustment was difficult to do with any accuracy. The best predictor of satisfaction and adjustment turned out to be the extent to which the expatriate's marital partner was happy with the move.

Family characteristics

The impact of international relocation on the family is not an area that has been extensively researched. What little that has been done has been concerned with adjustment among the partners (usually wives) of expatriate managers. That this is an important issue is reflected in the fact that a chapter of this book is dedicated to examining the problem of spouse adjustment.

The existing research is reasonably consistent in its conclusions: expatriate spouses tend to feel more socially and culturally isolated than their working partners; this sense of loss and isolation can lead to the feelings of anxiety and depression discussed in relation to culture shock; the extent to which spouses feel happy about an international move is the single most important factor in determining how satisfied expatriate managers are with their posting, and how successfully they adjust.

The reasons that underlie problems faced by spouses are looked at in detail in Chapter 3. Briefly, differences in adjustment are tied in with the different life styles adopted by managers and their partners. On arrival in a foreign country, the relocated employee has a job to go to. Apart from accounting for a large part of the manager's time, his or her job also provides some degree of familiarity, and colleagues with whom to share experiences and ask for help where needed.

Contrast this with the situation faced by the expatriate spouse. Typically, many will not be working. The first problem this creates is filling time. Boredom is an issue that many complain of. Second, not having a job can often deny a partner the opportunity of playing a significant or meaningful role in the family. The result may be a loss of self-esteem and feelings of worthlessness that often signal the onset of anxiety.

Those partners who occupy themselves with making domestic arrangements find themselves thrust into the thick of the new culture. As theories of culture shock point out, this can be a frustrating and even frightening experience, particularly where language and cultural differences are extreme. As frustration turns to anger, marital relationships come under increasing strain. It is not at all unusual for the relocated employee to feel guilty when faced with the obvious distress experienced by other family members. From this point, the cycle of guilt and anger can gather momentum until, faced with the possible breakdown of the family, the expatriate manager decides to abandon the assignment. The cost of early termination can be measured in financial terms from the employer's perspective, career damage terms from the manager's perspective, and psychological terms from the family's perspective. Avoiding such an outcome is evidently in the best interests of all concerned.

Predicting, in advance, which families are more or less likely to adapt successfully to an international relocation is no easier than making predictions concerning individual employees. However, that does not mean there are no practical lessons to be learned from the research findings.

During times of stress or strain, practical and emotional support from other people becomes very important. Expatriate managers often have a readily available source of this support in the shape of work colleagues. The same is evidently not true for their partners. As a result, many come to rely very heavily on the family for help. This is particularly evident during the early weeks of a foreign sojourn. Unfortunately, this period can often coincide with the expatriate manager having to work longer hours than usual in order to familiarize themselves with the foreign operation. For some, this may mean travelling extensively within the overseas territory. Where these trips mean spending nights away from home, spouses are further denied access to the most important, and in some cases, the only source of support available to them. Evidently it is in the best interests of all concerned if this situation can be avoided, especially during the first days and weeks of a foreign assignment.

This example provides a very simple illustration of the fundamental errors committed by researchers and practitioners alike when it comes to the issue of predicting successful adaptation to international relocation. There has been an undeniable tendency to attribute a failed international assignment to some weakness in either the individual employee or their family. The result has been a concerted effort to identify these potential weaknesses before a move is offered. The fundamental error of this enterprise is that the reasons for failure lie not in individual or family characteristics, but in characteristics of the move itself and the ways in which it is managed.

Findings from research into both domestic and international relocation need to be applied to the task of providing better relocation management rather than the hazardous pursuit of prediction and guesswork. To use an earlier example, the research findings on spouse adjustment should encourage organizations to keep marital separation to a minimum during the early period of an assignment. This is clearly more effective than trying to screen out, at the selection stage, partners likely to react badly to a move.

This principle will be developed in the next section, which looks at the practical implications of these issues for those charged with the responsibility of managing international mobility.

IMPLICATIONS FOR THE MANAGEMENT OF INTERNATIONAL MOBILITY

Selection

The point made in the previous section was that no matter how careful or rigorous selection procedures are, they are no guarantee of success or failure in the international mobility stakes. No single criterion, or collection of criteria, has been found to be an adequate predictor of successful adaptation. However, that does not mean that selection procedures should be entirely abandoned. What should be abandoned is the expectation that careful selection can completely eliminate expatriate failure.

As a general rule, candidates for international moves should not be selected for their technical ability alone. As the research findings have shown, adjustment to a foreign assignment involves much more than an ability to do the job on offer. An American study suggested that apart from technical ability, successful expatriates had a solid and positive belief in the reasons behind their move, an interest and understanding of politics, and demonstrated a sense of cultural empathy.

Above and beyond these general characteristics, other researchers claim that specific personality characteristics such as adaptability and emotional stability should be looked for. There are two main problems with this strategy. First, there are no reliable means of measuring complex patterns of behaviour that may or may not go to make up a trait such as "adaptability". Second, even when people have claimed to measure these things accurately, the measurements have proved unreliable in predicting the outcomes of international moves. Rather than attempt to be too specific at the selection stage, it makes more sense to concentrate on providing the best possible training prior to a move, and adequate support during the early days and weeks of a foreign assignment.

Training

In a review of international relocation practice among nine large multinational organizations with operations in the UK, Sue Shortland (1990), manager of the CBI's Employee Relocation Council, concludes that "companies are becoming more international in their outlook towards training".

Certainly there is some evidence to support that view. For example, Shell, the oil and gas conglomerate, has a policy of providing training in "intercultural communication" for all graduate entrants, irrespective of whether they are taking a foreign posting.

Most organizations provide language training for their employees prior to an international move. Some of the more forward thinking companies extend the same facility to spouses, and children where they are old enough. Given the importance of family adaptation to the success of a move, providing language classes for all involved is money well spent.

Cultural orientation is also something that many companies provide for potential expatriates and, in some cases, their families. Although this is more common where moves are intercontinental, training of this kind is now provided by some companies for employees moving within Europe.

More often than not, training of this kind is bought in from specialist providers such as the Centre for International Briefing (CIB), based in Surrey. However, the problem for employer organizations is deciding which methods of cultural orientation training are most effective. In their book *Culture Shock: Psychological Reactions to Unfamiliar Environments*, Furnham and Bochner (1986) provide a brief review and evaluation of some of the different techniques on offer.

Information giving

A simple exchange of information approach, even if done through the use of entertaining videos, lectures or slides, is rarely adequate. The main problem with this method is that the learners remain passive for the most part. It's a bit like trying to teach someone to drive without actually putting them behind the wheel of a car. The result is that while learners might remember the more exotic or entertaining facts they are given, there is no guarantee that they will be able to successfully adapt their behaviour to specific situations.

Cultural sensitization

Aimed at providing the learner with a greater appreciation of cultural differences, these courses often employ a compare and contrast approach. The first stage of the process is to arrive at an understanding of how one's own behaviour is intimately linked and influenced by indigenous culture. Once these principles have been established, the same process is applied to the links between a foreign culture and the behaviour of its citizens. In this way the learner comes to understand and appreciate the rituals, customs and culture of his or her proposed destination. However, the same criticisms as before can be levelled at this technique. Without active participation and practical experience, there is no guarantee that the information learned will influence behaviour once an employee is *in situ*.

Isomorphic attributions

Within our western culture, it is a fact that we have a tendency to attribute one set of reasons or causes to our own behaviour, and a different set to the same behaviour seen in others. For example, when I drive between lanes to beat a traffic jam, it is a legitimate means of saving time. When I see someone else doing the same thing I might attribute their behaviour to impatience.

When the two people involved in a similar interchange come from completely different cultures, there is an even greater chance that one will misunderstand the actions of the other. The idea behind this training method is to provide information about a foreign culture so that an outsider is more likely to understand the motives behind the behaviour they observe.

The technique often involves what is called a "cultural assimilator". Essentially this is a programmed learning manual which contains a series of example interchanges between the nationals of two different countries. Invariably these interchanges end in misunderstanding, embarrassment or hostility of some kind. The learner is asked to consider what went wrong, and to select, from a number of scenarios, an alternative that might have led to a more favourable outcome. Furnham and Bochner point out that this method, while actively involving the learner, tends to stand or fall on the choice of scenarios selected for training. While there is a temptation to use more interesting and thus more exotic examples, it is the more mundane, day-to-day exchanges that are likely to be of more practical use to potential expatriates.

Learning by doing

The advantages to be gained from active, rather than passive, learning have encouraged the development of training packages that involve learners in either real or simulated cross-cultural interchanges. These will usually involve role playing techniques, where trainers or actual members of the host culture will take on different roles in a variety of simulations. The performance of learners in each simulation is typically assessed by trained observers.

The disadvantage of this method concerns time and therefore money. While more effective than the information exchange methods, training through active participation can be more expensive.

Intercultural (social) skills training

Furnham and Bochner appear to favour a method of training tried and tested in the teaching of interactive skills such as assertiveness training, counselling, and social skills training. The technique typically involves a four-stage process: diagnosis of the problem, discussion and analysis of its elements or component parts, role play, and feedback.

The advantages of training via this method centre around the fact that it has been used to such good effect in other areas. There are sound theoretical justifications for the methods used, the emphasis is on teaching practical skills, attention is paid to the individual needs of learners, tried and tested methods of behaviour modification are used, it is focused on specific social skills, and has a built-in evaluative component. While more time consuming and therefore more costly than simple information exchange techniques, the implication is that providing courses of this kind may prove more cost effective in the long term.

Ongoing Support and "Open Door" Policies

Looking back to the theoretical work that has been done on processes of adjustment to international moves, the importance of ongoing support from employers is self-evident. The early days and weeks of an assignment are likely to be crucial to its long-term success. As employees and their families struggle with the inevitable consequences of culture shock, having someone to turn to for help is essential.

Some of the larger multinationals, such as the French pharmaceutical giant Rhône-Poulenc, arrange for expatriates to have direct and constant access to someone within the company personnel function. This so-called "open door" approach ensures that the expatriate has a source of support on whom they can call for help with a variety of difficulties, from accommodation to acclimatization.

Other strategies include the use of "buddy" systems, where an employee already established in the host nation will assume responsibility for an incoming colleague. This approach has the advantage of helping new arrivals to establish some kind of social network early on. Making new friends is an important step in adjusting to life in any novel environment.

Whether it be an "open door" or a "buddy" system, this kind of early support provides newcomers with a source of practical help, reassurance, and the knowledge that their experiences are not unique and can be coped with given time.

As with domestic relocation, provision of individual support of this kind is contingent on organizations being aware of the ongoing needs of their employees and families. There has to be some commitment on behalf of employers to canvass the views of expatriates and their dependants regularly. Unfortunately, this monitoring process is sometimes abandoned in the mistaken view that it amounts to no more than prying into people's private lives. On the contrary, for many relocatees it is a positive sign that the employing organization takes a healthy and helpful interest in their welfare during this turbulent time. From the organization's perspective, it enables help of the right kind to be offered in a pro-active fashion. Potential problems can be dealt with before they turn into crises that might jeopardize the whole assignment. That fact alone makes the provision of ongoing support a cost effective enterprise for organizations.

Finally, as pointed out earlier, families often come into their own during these potentially difficult times as sources of mutual support. However, this function can only operate successfully if the family has sufficient time to spend together. Evidently employees will be keen to familiarize themselves with the workings of a new business operation as soon as possible. The temptation is to work

longer hours than normal during the early stages of a foreign assignment. Organizations would be well advised to counsel employees
as to the importance of ensuring sufficient quality time with their
families, particularly through the first few weeks of a new posting.

Repatriation

Once the forgotten aspect of international relocation, repatriation
is something that most large organizations take very seriously.
Expatriates face adjustment on two fronts once they return to their
home country. The first is what some researchers have termed
"reverse culture shock". The second is the impact that spending
time away from the centre of an organization might have on the
expatriate's future career development.

The majority of expatriates return to their home country following
an international sojourn. Although they are coming back to a familiar
environment, an element of culture shock is inevitable. Apart from
the fact that things in the home country will have changed during
the period of absence, returning to a country with a different climate,
different culture and different living conditions can sometimes be
quite painful. The excitement of living abroad can make the home-
coming a disappointing and depressing experience. Adapting to
life back home can follow much the same pattern as the process of
adjusting to life in a foreign country described earlier.

The second issue facing employees on their return concerns their
future career with the organization. Shortland (1990) reported that
most of the companies she surveyed took an early and active interest in the returning expatriate's next job. The strategies vary from
one company to another. Some have a system whereby a manager's
whole career is the responsibility not just of the employee, but of a
"sponsor" as well. The sponsor therefore makes sure that the return
from overseas is marked by the availability of a suitable job, often
a promotion. In other organizations, a specialist from the personnel function will fulfil a similar role. Whatever the system in operation, plans to re-introduce the returning expatriate into the parent
company often take shape several months before the foreign
assignment is due to finish. This way potential problems are kept
to a minimum.

CONCLUSIONS

The growth of the global economy and the rise of large multinational organizations means that international relocation is set to become a more common feature of managerial life. Because of the costs involved, both human and financial, it is important that organizations get international job moves right. The research reviewed in this chapter suggests that the effects of culture shock, while to some extent inevitable, can be kept to a minimum through careful planning and effective policy. Trying to select which employees and families are more or less likely to adapt successfully to a foreign assignment has been characterized as little more than guesswork. More effective strategies concern the implementation of adequate training programmes, not just for employees, but for all those involved in an international move. Preparation and training then needs to be supplemented with ongoing support throughout the assignment, but particularly during the early weeks and months following arrival. Finally, the experience of most organizations has been that the principles of preparation and ongoing support need to be applied with equal diligence to repatriation, a part of the international mobility process which can also create difficulties for employees and their families.

CHAPTER 6 Conclusion: check-list for successful relocation

The previous chapters have taken a look at the personal side of relocation from a variety of perspectives. The aim has been to help those relocating, and those managing relocations, to understand the range of personal and family issues involved.

This final chapter provides, by way of a check-list, a summary of the points covered in each of the earlier chapters. The aim is to help individual relocatees and their families anticipate, and therefore cope with, the potential difficulties thrown up by a move.

FIRST PRINCIPLES

Moving home is becoming a much more common experience than was the case in generations past. In Britain, an estimated one in every three people moves home at least once every five years.

Moving home can be stressful. According to researchers, on a scale that has "death of a spouse" as the most stressful event anyone might experience (rated 100 on a scale of 0–100), change of residence scores 20. However, by understanding what makes moving home difficult for some people, the potential stresses of the situation can be reduced to a minimum.

The single most important point to remember when you and your family are faced with a move is that *people who plan their moves are much more likely to make a success of them*. Research into homesickness has shown that 52% of those who planned their moves adjusted successfully. This compares with only 24% among those who did not plan.

Should I Stay or Should I Go?

If a move is to be successful, it requires the enthusiastic commitment of everybody involved. Making the decision about whether or not to accept a relocation involves assessing your commitment to your current location. It involves what economists might call a cost/benefit analysis. Do the costs of relocating outweigh the benefits?

Evidently the costs associated with relocating include elements other than straightforward financial ones. But what are they and how are they assessed? As a first stage, examine what is important in your life, where your present commitments lie. There are a number of ways of doing this. Thinking of general headings is often a useful place to start. Most people can divide their lives into at least three categories: family life, work life and social life. Next, look at each category in turn, and think about the things that you might include under that heading.

The survey of relocating families referred to earlier in the book reported that 70% experienced stress due to family disruption. Family life is an extremely important area of most people's lives, one that they are extremely committed to. There are a variety of potential disruptions to family life that need to be considered prior to a move. Children's education and their ability to make new friends comes high on most people's lists.

In many families today, both marriage partners have careers. Dual career couples are becoming more the rule rather than the exception. A partner obliged to make a move that is not in their own best career interests is less likely to be fully committed to that move. This can have serious implications for the ability of the family to adjust to a new environment. Other factors to consider include possible effects on the extended family. Will the move mean living further away from elderly relatives? How committed is the family to its current location? How will the relocation influence overall quality of life for all concerned?

Work is very important for a variety of reasons. On a material level, it provides the financial means of support for ourselves and our families. On a more psychological level, it is a source of satisfaction, of a feeling of self-esteem or self-worth. Many people use their job description when defining their place in society. "What do you do?" is a question that often crops up in conversations between new acquaintances. For all these reasons, commitment to work is often very strong.

For most people, relocation usually goes hand in hand with promotion. This often presents the employee with a dilemma: balancing commitment to work with commitment to the family. The choice is rarely an easy one. While a move may be disruptive in the short term, the resulting financial gains may provide greater long-term security for the whole family.

Commitment to social life is no less important. Having friends, belonging to clubs or organizations and pursuing interests and hobbies all contribute towards our psychological health. Giving these things up may be too great a cost. On the benefit side, a move doesn't have to mean giving up your favourite pastime. Sports and leisure facilities aren't necessarily unique to your present location. Indeed, the move may give you the chance to take up new leisure interests.

Thinking carefully about commitment to family, work and social aspects of your life is essential before deciding on a move. Communicating those thoughts to the rest of the family, and encouraging them to talk about their own commitments, is no less important. Not everybody finds it an easy exercise, but it is one that can be extremely rewarding, regardless of the final decision on moving.

In the first of three case studies taken from our research files we examine the situation of a family of four faced with a move from the North of England to South Wales. This typical example covers many of the issues involved in the process of making the decision about whether to accept a transfer when the whole family is involved.

Case study 1

Michael works for a large glass manufacturer. Since joining the company as a graduate, he has worked in the same plant for 12 years. Over the past few months, Michael has become aware that if he is to be promoted, he will have to transfer to another of the company's sites. Not long ago, it came to his attention that a vacancy was due to come up at a plant in South Wales. To his delight, he has been offered the post. However, should he accept it, it will involve moving himself and his family some 250 miles away from their current location.

The first decision facing Michael is whether or not to accept the job offer. He begins the process by talking it over with his wife, Jill, and, later on, with the two children, Peter (aged 8) and Sally (aged 6).

Evidently the financial gains to be made through Michael's promotion would benefit the whole family. However, the first issue is the children's education. Both Peter and Sally are happy at their respective schools, although Sally has had a few difficulties recently. Jill and Michael have put these down to the fact that since her class teacher left, Sally has been taught by several replacements this year. In any event, neither of the children are at a particularly crucial stage in terms of examinations just now. However, Jill would like some assurance that they won't be asked to move again in a few years' time when the children would be at a more important phase of their education.

Jill works as a departmental manager in a large store. Her career is very important to her, and to the family budget. After discussing the possibilities of a transfer with her company, she has the offer of a sideways move to a branch in South Wales. There is no immediate prospect of promotion, but there again there is no certainty of a better position if she stays where she is.

— *continued* —

continued

Michael and Jill have lived in the same town for nearly 12 years. Not surprisingly, they have built up quite a large circle of friends, not to mention the baby-sitters. The children also have several friends who live close by. This is a serious sticking point. Having to leave their friends makes Jill, in particular, feel very sad. It has taken her a long time to get to know people, particularly her two closest friends that live near by. She points out to Michael that he is much more outgoing than her, and consequently tends to find it easier to meet and talk to new people. However, Michael has discovered that there is a branch of the National Childbirth Trust (NCT), of which Jill is a member, not far from where they may move to. He reassures Jill that she will make some new contacts through NCT, and that he will look after the children at least two nights each week so that she can enrol in the art classes she has been talking about for ages. Peter and Sally have been involved with Cubs and Brownies for some time. They shouldn't have too much trouble joining new packs. It would certainly be a good way for them to meet new friends.

Neither Michael nor Jill has any other family in their present town. In fact, given that both sets of parents live in the South West, a move to Wales would make visiting them that much easier.

After a great deal of discussion, the family decide that a move would be the best thing all round. Michael accepts the job offer and is given a starting date three months hence.

YOU AND YOUR EMPLOYER

So, you've made the decision to relocate. What kind of help can you expect from your employer? The simple answer is: it depends. The range of benefits and remunerations offered to relocating employees varies considerably from one commercial or industrial sector to the next. Furthermore, the circumstances surrounding a move can influence the type of relocation package offered. A good description of what the "typical" relocation package consists of can be found in Shortland (1990).

Whatever your employer may or may not provide, there are certain questions that you need to ask in order to make sure you get the best from whatever is on offer. These questions can be divided into two crude categories: aspects specific to your change of job, and aspects more specific to the move. For example, these are a few of the questions you might want to ask:

1. *Your job change*

- Whom do I talk to if I have questions about my change of job?

- Where can I get an accurate job preview?

- Will I need further training for my new post?

- Is there any kind of planned hand-over period with the previous incumbent?

- How much time do I have to wind up my old job?

- What are the expectations concerning settling into the new post?

- How long before I can expect to move again?

2. *Your move*

- Whom can I talk to if things get difficult or complicated?

- Who will talk to my partner?

- How flexible is the relocation package?

- What provisions are there for keeping the family together over the course of the move?

- To what extent can I control the timing of the move?

- What happens if I can't sell my house?

- How much time do I have to look for a new place?

Questions such as those listed above are a useful way of helping your employer to help you and your family. If your problems and anxieties remain a well kept secret, you are less likely to get help with them. Getting these issues out in the open right from the start of the relocation process is better for all concerned. It means that you and your family will settle into your new location that much more quickly. The faster you all feel at home, the more effective you are likely to be when it comes to work.

The second of our case histories looks at the way in which one young couple were able to move with few major hassles. Their move was relatively successful because of the flexible approach of their respective employers, and the "open door" policy adopted by both personnel professionals and line managers.

Case study 2

Graham and Julie have been married for three years. They plan to have children later, but want to establish their respective careers first. Julie is a systems analyst for a large bank. She has been offered a move to another city as part of her career development programme. Both Julie and Graham expected to have to move around quite a bit during the early years of their marriage, which is one of the reasons they are waiting before they start a family.

The timing of the move and the changes involved in Julie's work duties have been explained by her line manager. He has made a point of telling her that his door is open any time she wants to discuss things. Someone in Personnel has already explained the terms and conditions of the relocation package on offer to both Julie and Graham. Graham works in the wholesale distribution trade. He has arranged a transfer to the new location and can start almost immediately.

The relocation package includes payment for the services of a relocation management company. They operate a guaranteed sale price scheme that has the effect of making

continued

┌─ *continued* ─────────────────────────────

Julie and Graham first-time buyers in the new location. However, there have been a few problems, the main one being that Julie felt the relocation company were seriously undervaluing her house. With all the other hassles of moving, they were not at all pleased when they were offered a few thousand pounds less than they had anticipated. In the end, a compromise was reached between Julie's bank and the relocation management company, but she and Graham felt that the whole issue could have been handled with a little more sensitivity.

With both of them working quite long hours to begin with, finding a suitable place to buy is taking a little time. Normally, Julie's employer pays for temporary hotel accommodation for up to three months while the hunt for a permanent place goes on. However, with their two cats, living in a hotel would be inconvenient for the couple. Fortunately, Julie's contact in Personnel knows about this problem, and arranges for the company to pay for unfurnished rented accommodation as an alternative. This has the added benefit that Graham and Julie don't have the bother of storing their furniture, and have the comfort of their familiar possessions around them.

EARLY DAYS

Given that moving involves a separation from familiar surroundings, it is perhaps not surprising that, for some, the effects can be similar to bereavement. This can sometimes lead to the development of unpleasant emotional and physical complaints.

However, it is also evident that many people cope with moving very well. Those that move frequently often express greater satisfaction with marital and family relationships. The business of moving can bring couples and families closer together. Evidently the effects a move may have on the family will vary. The desirability of the move, the degree of control that the family has over the timetable of events and the acceptability of the final destination are all crucial elements.

For many parents considering a move, their main worries are about possible effects on their children. Specific concerns are educational development, and the ability of children to establish new friendships. Research suggests that in both of these areas, it is older, adolescent children who are more likely to experience difficulties. Many children in the 13–14 age group and above are involved in examination courses that have a bearing on their adult careers. Quite rightly, parents are often reluctant to move if their children are at such a critical stage. However, there is no consistent evidence to suggest that frequent moves among younger children have any long-term effects on educational development. Indeed some parents report that a move has resulted in their taking a much greater interest in their child's schooling, a good thing for all involved. Similarly, adolescent children may experience some difficulties in making new friends. Peer groups at this age tend to be very close-knit. New arrivals may find it hard to break into these groups initially.

Reducing the stress of a move to a minimum is within the reach of everybody. It requires only a knowledge of potential problems and careful planning. Planning is something that has to start from the moment the possibility of a move becomes apparent.

Stress is less likely in situations where people feel they have *control* over events. For this reason, it is important that the whole family becomes involved in the move as early as possible. Informing partners and children as to what is happening on a "need to know" basis is often a recipe for disaster.

The transition to a new environment will be easier for those people committed to moving. *Commitment* is more likely to follow when those involved feel that they have had a say in the move.

Finally, *communication* is essential. It is almost inevitable that some members of the family will experience some sense of loss or upset. For example, research shows that 60%–70% of university students experience homesickness in their first year. In order to provide a supportive environment, family members need to be able to talk freely about the problems they may encounter. If talking about the move has been encouraged from the planning stage, a valuable source of help and support has been established (see Table 6.1).

Table 6.1. Minimizing disruption

Psychologists suggest that there are three crucial elements to making the process of moving home as trouble free as possible: commitment, communication, control.

Here are a few practical suggestions:

Commitment

- Display a street map of the new town to familiarize your family with areas and districts
- Take the family on regular visits where possible
- Identify recreational amenities such as parks, swimming pools and bowling alleys
- Establish contact with local branches of any national organizations to which you belong
- Investigate local history, places of historical interest
- Subscribe to local papers/publications

Communication

- Involve the family in discussions about the move
- Keep a special time, perhaps after evening meals, when people have an opportunity to express their feelings
- Encourage individuals to talk about any worries they may have
- Help family members to recognize that feeling sad or a sense of loss is quite common and acceptable
- Make lists of the positive aspects of moving to the new location

Control

- Tell the family about an impending move as soon as possible.
- Create an atmosphere of discussion in which each family member feels able to make some contribution.
- Let family members have their say about the kind of new house they would like to live in.
- Give children the freedom to choose how they would like their room decorated.
- Give individuals move-related jobs or tasks to do.
- Encourage family members to think of activities for weekend visits or leisure time after the move has been made.
- Try to let children take an active role in their choice of new school.

SEARCHING FOR A HOUSE AND SETTLING IN

The most common source of pre-move worry concerns finding the right house. A methodical approach to the job of choosing a new home can often help.

A move is often an opportunity to upgrade living accommodation. For many people the aim is to find a new place that retains some features of the old home, but at the same time represents an improvement. To help in the process of deciding what features you would like your new home to have, make a list of things about your existing house that you like, followed by a list of things that you would like to change. For example, proximity to local amenities may be fine, but a new baby in the family may mean having an extra bedroom. Different family members may have different ideas. Involving them in discussions can help fire their enthusiasm for the relocation (see Table 6.2).

One obvious factor influencing the desirability of a house concerns the neighbourhood in which it stands. Physical environment has an obvious impact on our lives. Proximity to local schools, leisure facilities, ease of access to the local commercial centre and availability of public transport are all important. When you've found a neighbourhood you think you like, remember to take a look at it at different times of the day. A place that is quiet during a weekday afternoon may be very different on a Saturday evening. Looking around a house during the day, while the amateur rock musician next door is at work, can lead to unpleasant surprises later on.

Equally important is the social feel of a new neighbourhood. An American survey reported that 70% of people moving house found their neighbours to be an important element in helping them to feel welcome in a new community. Think about the kind of people that live in the new area. Are they the type of people that you and your family are likely to get on with? Research shows that when neighbours are seen as unfriendly, there is a much greater tendency to report problems with settling in to a new area.

The loss of familiar surroundings and friendly faces can, like any loss, be traumatic. Stress researchers agree that friends are a valuable source of help during these periods. Unfortunately, moving house often means losing this resource. Many families cope by providing each other with support, becoming self-sufficient for a while.

Rebuilding a new life in a new location is evidently a priority. The aim is to get the family settled as quickly and painlessly as possible. This involves stabilizing the family environment, re-introducing familiarity. When asked about things that helped them to feel settled

Table 6.2. Looking for a new home

The job of finding a new home can be one of the most difficult facing the relocating family. It is a decision that you will literally have to live with. For most of us it is the biggest single purchase we ever make. How can you avoid buying a house that does not really suit your needs? How do you choose between one house and another? How can you make an objective decision in the face of a persuasive estate agent?

The answer is *be prepared*.

It is unlikely that you will want to find an exact replica of the house you are moving from. For many people circumstances change between moves. Income may increase, the family may grow.

(a) Preparing for a house search involves a number of simple stages:

1.	Your present home	Get each family member to list all the positive and negative aspects
2.	Your new home	Using list 1, each family member can note down desired features
3.	A weighting system	In consultation with the family, give each item from your lists of priorities a weighting. For example, if having four bedrooms is very important, it would receive a weighting of 100. If having two bathrooms would be nice but not vital, it might get a weighting of 20

(b) Using this system gives a matrix like this:

	House A	House B	House C	House D
Four bedrooms (weighting 100)	×	×		×
A garden (80)		×	×	
Twenty minutes travelling time from work (70)	×	×		
Walking distance from local school (70)		×	×	×
Local shopping facilities (60)	×		×	×
Fitted kitchen (50)	×	×	×	×
North of the city (50)		×	×	×
No redecoration required (30)	×		×	
A garage (20)		×		
Two bathrooms (20)		×	×	
Totals	310	460	360	330

in after a move, 86% of people responding to a survey said the arrival of furniture and other familiar objects was the most important first step. Second on the list was the return to a normal family schedule. Re-introducing regular mealtimes, family leisure activities and bedtimes can all help.

Making new friends is extremely important for many people. For the more extrovert it can be a relatively simple process. However, there are a number of strategies that can be used by everybody wanting to make new contacts. Work usually provides the first, but by no means the only opportunity. Members of national organizations, such as the Rotary Club, can join local branches. The church can fulfil a similar role for many others. Children can provide informal occasions for meeting people: collecting children from school or attending PTA meetings, for example. Even attending evening classes to learn that language you always wanted to speak can help.

However nice your new house, or however friendly your new neighbours, some feelings of homesickness are inevitable. They are most likely to occur in short episodes, becoming less frequent as time goes by. This is quite a normal reaction, and needs to be dealt with sensitively by family members. Researchers suggest that keeping busy is an effective way of reducing feelings of homesickness. Active leisure pursuits, and not too many visits home, to begin with, also help.

The final case history illustrates how each relocation can throw up its own idiosyncratic problems. Even for the most well-travelled of families, novel complications must be dealt with. Having a well-rehearsed routine can keep much of the disruption to a minimum, but that always leaves the unexpected.

Case study 3

For years, relocation has been part of John and Peggy's way of life. John's climb up the ladder in the financial services sector has meant moving around once every two to three years. They reckon this move makes it about twelve relocations in the last 26 years. Hopefully this will be the last time, although that's what John said as he broke the news on the previous occasion.

continued

---

continued

Despite the frequency with which they have moved in the past, relocating never seems to get easier. Each time is different. Each move throws up its unique problems. This time the complication involves the eldest of John and Peggy's two daughters. Karen is 22 years old, and has just finished a university degree in textile design. She has been offered a job locally, and so has decided that she won't be moving with the family this time. John and Peggy knew the time would come sooner or later, but it makes the move that much more of a hurdle.

As usual, on receiving news of the impending relocation, the family swings into action like a well-organized machine. A map of the new area is on the kitchen wall, and a pile of brochures from the local tourist office, the Chamber of Commerce, leisure services department, and goodness knows who else, awaits inspection.

Two possible areas have been identified as having potential. One is just south of the city centre, offering good access to the motorway. John will still have to cover quite a lot of territory in his new post, so proximity to the motorway network is important. The other possibility is one of two small villages further away from the city. Both are close to a large water sports complex, ideal for a family with a passion for sailing.

Sarah, the younger daughter, has just left sixth-form college. She is interested in a business course at a specialist college in the city centre. Living out in one of the villages would present some problems for her. Public transport services have been reduced to a minimum in that area. However, given that Sarah has passed her driving test, John could compromise by helping her to buy a car.

Following intense discussion, the ideal criteria for the new house is arrived at. With only three of them living in the house, the place doesn't need to be as big as their current home. However, a minimum of three bedrooms is

continued

continued

a requirement. Peggy runs an interior design consultancy from home, so needs one reasonably large room in which to work. Add to that the necessity of keeping a small sailing dinghy somewhere, and the ideal home begins to take shape.

Through a process of consultation and compromise, the move will go as smoothly as can be expected. There will be some inevitable upset and anxiety, but the family have been through the process before and know how to spot potential problems and how to help each other work them out. Regular discussions are a vital part of the process.

REFERENCES
AND FURTHER READING

Adler, N. (1981). Re-entry: Managing cross-cultural transitions. *Group and Organisational Studies*, **6**, 341–356.

Adler, N.J. (1991). *International Dimensions of Organizational Behaviour*, 2nd edition. Kent Publishing Company.

Adler, P. (1975). The transition experience: An alternative view of culture shock. *Journal of Humanistic Psychology*, **15**, 13–23.

Barry, A. (1990). Trade unions prepare for 1992. *Involvement and Participation*, **4**, 5–9.

Black, J. (1988). Work-role transitions: A study of American expatriate managers in Japan. *Journal of International Business Studies*, **19**, 227–294.

Black, J. (1990). The relationship of personal characteristics with the adjustment of Japanese expatriate managers. *Management International Review*, **30**, 119–134.

Black, J. and Gregersen, H. (1991). Antecedents to cross-cultural adjustment for expatriates in Pacific rim assignments. *Human Relations*, **44**(5), 497–515.

Black, J. and Mendenhall, M. (1990). Cross-cultural training effectiveness: A review and a theoretical framework for future research. *Academy of Management Review*, **15**(1), 113–136.

Black, J. and Porter, L. (1991). Managerial behaviours and job performance: A successful manager in Los Angeles may not succeed in Hong Kong. *Journal of International Business Studies*, **15**, 99–113.

Black, J. and Stephens, G. (1989). The influence of the spouse on American expatriate adjustment in overseas assignments. *Journal of Management*, **15**, 529–544.

Black, J., Mendenhall, M. and Oddou, G. (1991). Towards a comprehensive model of international adaptation: An integration of multiple theoretical perspectives. *Academy of Management Review*, **16**(2), 291–318.

Brett, J. (1980). The effect of job transfer on employees and their families. In C. Cooper and R. Payne (eds) *Current Concerns in Occupational Stress*. Wiley.

Brett, J., Stroh, L. and Reilly, A. (1990). *Impact of Societal Shifts and Corporate Changes on Employee Relocation*. Employee Relocation Council.

Brewster, C. and Myers, A. (1989). *Managing the Global Manager: New Research Data*. The Cranfield School of Management.

Cagney, W. (1975). Executive re-entry: The problems of repatriation. *Personnel Journal*, September, 487–488.

Cooper, C. (1979). *The Executive Gypsy: The Quality of Managerial Life*. Macmillan.

Cooper, C. and Fisher, S. (eds) (1990). *On the Move*. Wiley.

Cooper, C. and Makin, P. (1985). The mobile managerial family. *Journal of Management Development*, **4**(3), 56–66.

Cooper, C.L., Cooper, R.D. and Eaker, L.H. (1988). *Living with Stress*. Penguin.

Copeland, L. and Griggs, L. (1985). *Going International*. Random House.

Croft, P. (1991). Companies need to have a global perspective. *Personnel Management*, May, 16.

Forster, N. (1990). A practical guide to the management of job changes and relocation. *Personnel Review*, **19**(4), 26–35.

Forster, N. (1991a). Developing the role of the personnel function in the management of job mobility. *Human Resource Management Journal*, October.

Forster, N. (1991b). Employee job mobility and relocation: a major challenge for human resource managers in the 1990s. *Personnel Review*, **19**(6), 18–24.

Forster, N. and Munton, A.G. (1990). Managing the personal side of relocation. *BPS Guidance and Assessment Review*, **6**, 4–7.

Forster, N. and Munton, A.G. (1991). The danger of a false move. *Personnel Management*, January, 40–43.

Furnham, A. and Bochner, S. (1986). *Culture shock: Psychological Reactions to Unfamiliar Environments*. Methuen.

Greenbury, L.R. (1988). Relocating the working wife. *Relocation News*, **5**, 3–5.

Greenbury, L.R. (1990a). Relocating single women abroad and at home. *Relocation News*, 13.

Greenbury, L.R. (1990b). Young, female and willing to travel. *Careers International*, 4.

Hamill, J. (1989). Expatriate policies in British multi-nationals. *Journal of General Management*, **14**, 18–33.

Harvey, M. (1982). The other side of foreign assignments: dealing with the repatriation dilemma. *Columbia Journal of World Business*, **17**, 53–59.

Hiltrop, J.-M. and Janssens, M. (1990). Expatriation: challenges and recommendations. *European Management Journal*, **8**(1), 19–26.

Hofstede, G. (1980). *Culture's Consequences*. Sage Publications.

Holden, N. (1989). Language, customer closeness and the concept of communication competence: empirical descriptions of industrial firms' interactions in contrasting foreign markets. Unpublished manuscript. (Available from: The Management School, University of Manchester Institute of Management and Technology.)

Howard, C. (1974). The returning overseas executive; culture shock in reverse. *Human Resource Management*, **13**(2), 22–26.

Institute for Manpower Studies (1987). Relocating managers and professional staff. Report No. 139, Institute for Manpower Studies.

Johnston, J. (1991). An empirical study of the repatriation of managers in UK multinationals. *Human Resource Management Journal*, **1**(4), 102–109.

Legge, K. (1978). *Power, Innovation and Problem Solving in Personnel Management*. McGraw-Hill.

Legge, K. (1989). Human resource management: a critical analysis. In J. Storey (ed.) *New Perspectives on Human Resource Management*. Routledge.

Luo, L. and Cooper, C. (1990). Stress of job relocation: progress and prospect. *Work and Stress*, **4**(2), 121–128.

McCullum, A. (1990). *The Trauma of Moving: Psychological Issues for Women*. Sage Publications.

McLoughlin, J. (1990). *The Demographic Revolution*. Faber.

Merril Lynch (1988). Fifth annual study of employee relocation policies among UK companies. (Available from: Merril Lynch Relocation Management International, 136 New Bond Street, London WIY 9FA.)

Mole, J. (1989). *Mind Your Manners: Culture Clash in the Single European Market*. IS Press.

Munton, A. (1990). Job relocation, stress and the family. *Journal of Organisational Behaviour*, **11**, 401–406.

Munton, A. (1991). *Managerial Job Relocation and Stress: A Two-Year Investigation* (Available from: The MRC/ESRC Social and Applied Psychology Unit, The University of Sheffield, price £50.)

Munton, A. and Forster, N. (1990). Job relocation: stress and the role of the family, *Work and Stress*, **4**(1), 75–81.

Nicholson, N. and West, M. (1988). *Managerial Job Change: Men and Women in Transition*. Cambridge University Press.

Phatak, A.V. (1974). *Managing Multinational Corporations*. Praeger Publishers.

Pinder, C. (1989). The dark side of executive relocation. *Organisational Dynamics*, **17**, 48–58.

Pinder, M. (1990). *Personnel Management for the Single European Market*. Pitman.

Price Waterhouse and CBI Employee Relocation Council (1989). *Moving Experiences*. Price Waterhouse and CBI Employee Relocation Council.

Shortland, S. (1988). *Managing Relocation*. Macmillan.

Shortland, S. (1989). International relocation, paper presented at the 11th CBI/ERC Conference, 6th October. (Available from: The CBI/ERC, Centre Point, 103 New Oxford Street, London WC1A 1DU.)

Shortland, S.M. (1990). *Relocation: A Practical Guide*. IPM.

Smith, A. (1991). Not such splendid isolation. *Industrial Society Magazine*, March, 9–12.

Sperl, R. (1988). Cross-border transfers of employees: an expensive business, paper presented at the 4th CBI/ERC International Conference, 1st March. (Available from: The CBI/ERC, Centre Point, 103 New Oxford Street, London WC1A 1DU.)

Stephens, G. and Black, S. (1991). The impact of spouses' career orientation on managers during international transitions. *Journal of Management Studies*, **28**(4), 417–428.

Storey, J. (ed.) (1989). *New Perspectives on Human Resource Management*. Routledge.

Trompenaars, F. (1991). The single market involves huge cultural problems. *Personnel Management*, May, 17.

Tung, R. (1982). Selection and training procedures of US, European and Japanese multinationals. *California Management Review*, **25**(1), 57–71.

Tung, R. (1984). *Key to Japan's Economic Strength: Human Power.* Lexington Books.

Tung, R. (1988a) *The New Expatriates: Managing Human Resources Abroad.* Ballinger.

Tung, R. (1988b). Career issues in international assignments. *Academy of Management Executive*, **11**, 241–244.

Wood, S. and Peccei, R. (1991). Preparing for 1992: Business versus strategic human resource management. *Human Resource Management Journal*, **1**(1), 63–89.

SELECTED
FURTHER INFORMATION

INFORMATION/CAREER COUNSELLING CENTRES:

Access, Bezuidenhoutseweg 125E, 2594 GN Den Haag, The Netherlands (Tel: 31.070.383.6161).

Career Development Centre for Women, 97 Mallard Place, Strawberry Vale, Twickenham, Middlesex TW1 4SW, UK (Tel: 081 892 3806).

Catlyst, 250 Park Avenue South, New York, NY 10003, USA.

Focus Career Centre, "The Metairie", 19 Kattenberg, 1170 Brussels, Belgium (Tel: 32.02.672.3408).

Focus Information Services, 22–23 Kensington Gardens Square, London W2 4BE, UK (Tel: 071 221 9600).

WICE, 20 bd du Montparnasse, 75015 Paris, France (Tel: 45.66.75.50).

Women's Corona Society, Minster House, 275 Vauxhall Bridge Road, London SW1V 1BB, UK (Tel: 071 828 1652/3).

NETWORK GROUPS:

Note: Network groups may be formally or informally organized, "in house" and/or run by volunteers with fast changing officials and addresses. The following are up to date at the time of writing. Check for alterations with the Equal Opportunities Commission, Overseas House, Quay Street, Manchester M3 3HN, UK (Tel: 061 833 9244).

British Council Wives and Husbands Association, PM Division, The British Council, 65 Davies Street, London W1, UK.

Business Women's Travel Club, 520 Fulham Road, London SW6 5NJ, UK (Tel: 071 384 1121).

Diplomatic Service Wives Association (contact the Foreign and Commonwealth Office).

European Women's Management Development Network, UK Representative, Geraldine Bown, Domino Training Ltd, 56 Charnwood Road, Shepshed, Leicestershire LE12 9NP, UK.

Federation of Army Wives (contact United Kingdom Land Forces).

Federation of Business and Professional Women, 23 Ansdell Street, London W8 5BN, UK (Tel: 071 938 1729).

National Women's Register, National Office, 9 Bank Plain, Norwich NR2 4SL, UK (Tel: 0603 765392).

Women Returners Network, Gloria Walling, Development Officer, 100 Park Village East, London NW1, UK (Tel: 071 387 2171).

Working Mothers Association, 77 Holloway Road, London N7 8JZ, UK (Tel: 071 700 5771).

BOOKS:

Self-assessment:

Bastress, F. (1986). *The Relocating Spouse's Guide to Employment.* Woodley Publications.

Bolles, R. (1991). *What Color is Your Parachute?* Ten Speed Press.

Hopson, B. and Scally, M. (1984). *Build Your Own Rainbow.* Lifeskills Associates.

Willis, E. and Daisley, J. (1990). *Springboard Women's Development Book.* Hawthorn Press.

Others:

Griffith, S. (1991). *Teaching English Abroad.* Vacation Work.

Honychurch, R.R. and Battles, H.K. (1991). *The Complete Relocation Kit.* Dearborn Financial Publishing Inc.

Piet-Pelon, N.J. and Hornby, B. (1986). *Women Overseas: A Practical Guide.* Institute of Personnel Management.

Shaevitz, M. (1984). *The Superwoman Syndrome.* Collins/Fontana.

Velmans, M. and Litvinoff, S. (1987). *Working Mother: A Practical Handbook.* Corgi.

INDEX

Index compiled by Geoffrey C. Jones